Wayne Van Ki

in memory of

Mrs. K. H. Elving

died November 11, 1948

RESURGENCE OF THE GOSPEL

RESURGENCE
OF THE GOSPEL

By T. A. KANTONEN

THE MUHLENBERG PRESS — PHILADELPHIA

To the memory of my mother
who built a home upon the Rock

CONTENTS

FOREWORD

THIS BOOK is the outgrowth of lectures delivered by the author at the Midwinter Convocation of Luther Seminary, St. Paul, Minnesota, January 28-31, 1947. In the present form these lectures have been expanded and documented to about twice their original length and the final chapter has been added to indicate the practical application of the theological principles set forth. Portions of the content have also been orally presented to pastors' conferences at Detroit, Michigan; Hancock, Michigan; Toledo, Ohio; Bedford, Pennsylvania; and Columbia, South Carolina. The criticism and the encouragement received from these pastoral groups, representing all branches of American Lutheranism, is cheerfully acknowledged. My thanks are also due to the publishers mentioned in the references for permission to quote from their works and especially to the Augsburg Publishing House for relinquishing the publication rights to the original lectures.

The responsibility for the views expressed here rests with the author alone. This should be borne in mind especially in reading Chapter III, in which, as throughout, I have sought to follow faithfully the lead of

Luther, but recognize the wide prevalence of divergent views among Lutherans.

In quoting Scripture I have used the Revised Standard Version of the New Testament wherever it appears to convey more clearly the meaning of the Word.

While this is a work in Lutheran theology, its scope does not permit a systematic presentation of the whole round of the Church's doctrine. Nor is it meant to be a book only for pastors. Intelligent laymen are more interested in theology and more capable of grasping it than pastors tend to realize. If this book will help to focus attention upon the vitality and perennial relevance of the basic truths of the evangelical faith, its purpose will be achieved.

T. A. KANTONEN

Springfield, Ohio.

CHAPTER I

THE CONTEMPORARY THEOLOGICAL SCENE

BY THE LIGHT of burning cities, set on fire by atomic bombs, a new day has dawned for mankind. What are the basic convictions which guide into this new day the people who live by the Gospel of Christ? That is the question which underlies this study of theology in the contemporary scene.

The use of the term "theology" should not lead anyone to presume that such an inquiry can interest only the professionally religious who are compelled to give some thought to the theoretical aspects of religion. As a recent editorial in a popular weekly magazine expressed it, "Everyone who thinks at all about the universe, morals, and the destiny of man is a theologian. Modern man has not abandoned this archscience; he has simply fallen into incredibly careless and sloppy ways of pursuing it."[1]

The charge made in the latter half of this statement does not apply to representative Lutheran theology. On the contrary, the simplicity and vitality of its foundation-principles have often been obscured by the pains-

---

[1] *Life,* December 23, 1946, p. 24.

takingly precise and elaborate superstructure which our theologians have erected upon them. Lutheranism cannot properly be identified with any set of propositions nor even with any group of congregations. It is the spirit of receptivity and loyalty to the Gospel, wherever that spirit may exist. It is as universal and as dynamic as the grace of God which is the heart of its proclamation. Our main task will be to show the relevance of such an emphasis to the world today. Before undertaking it, however, it will be necessary to sketch as its background the contemporary theological situation in general as it appears in the American perspective. Let us study, then (1) the theological scene today as compared with the scene at the end of the first World War, (2) the basic direction of contemporary theology, and (3) the central themes of theological thinking today.

I. TWO SCENES

Amid the din which accompanied the end of the first World War the sound given forth by the trumpet of American theology was thin as well as uncertain. Natural science was the established sovereign in the realm of thought, and the leading theologians of the day had become accustomed to picking up the crumbs that fell from the table of the scientists. In the effort to square Christianity with science, God was interpreted to be an immanent world-process of which one could say, "Some call it Evolution, and others call it God." Tennyson's little flower from the crannies was held in very truth

to be the key to "what God and man is." American
religious liberals, usually called "modernists," following
the trail blazed by Adolf Harnack's *What is Christianity?*, preferred the alleged simple moral religion *of* Jesus
to the later complicated religion *about* Jesus. The
attempt was to brush aside all the centuries of theolo-
gizing about the Christ of faith ever since Paul and to
take one's place among the listeners of the prophet of
Nazareth on some Galilean mountainside or lake shore
as He expounded the timeless ethical principles which
would stir to life the latent divinity in every decent
man. The historic confessions of the Church therefore
had to give way to new creeds professing faith in the
fatherhood of God, the brotherhood of man, the leadership of Jesus, salvation by character, and the upward
and onward progress of the human race. The most advanced liberals, the humanists, denied the very existence of God beyond man's own social and moral aspirations. The theistic modernists, as well as the humanists,
either ridiculed or ignored the idea of supernatural
revelation. Theology, once queen of the sciences, had
no realm of her own and had to seek employment at
the doors of such newcomers as sociology and philosophy of religion. The defense of revealed orthodox
Christianity was undertaken by groups of devout Christian men called "fundamentalists." The effectiveness of
their service, however, was seriously curtailed by their
violent bibliolatry which rejected even the constructive
results of biblical criticism and by their strong anti-

scientific bias which alienated all but the unthinking
and the uneducated. To theological study as such the
fundamentalists could contribute little if anything, for
their method of categorical pronouncement on the basis
of uncritically accepted external authority, coupled with
a vehement castigation of all who disagreed, precluded
any open-minded inquiry.

As the deeper implications of the war came into a
distinct focus, and the bright hope of a world made
safe for peace and democracy faded into the gray light
of postwar disillusionment, the inadequacy of the prevailing forms of theology to meet the realities of the
day became more and more manifest. If the fundamentalists were seen to defend the citadel of faith with
antiquated weapons, the modernists, who had left the
citadel behind to venture forth on far-flung fields of
conquest, were still worse off. They had suffered a
crushing defeat. Their dream of a Kingdom of God,
born out of faith in evolutionary social progress and
supported by faith in the goodness of man, had been
rudely shattered. Social enthusiasm had found more
than its match in the terrifying depths of evil revealed
in human nature. Science had proved itself a poor ally,
for its lack of any inherent spiritual quality had come
to light as it debased itself into an instrument of evil.
The whole modernistic outlook had turned out to be an
untenable halfway house between supernatural religion
and a frankly naturalistic humanism. It could not meet
the demands either of theological scholarship or of

religious life. Biblical research, using such method as form-criticism, showed the simple Galilean mo... teacher to be a figment of modern imagination while the Jesus of history actually proclaimed an eschatological kingdom. As to the needs of the practical religious life, a young American minister wrote from the battle-front in France in 1918: "I have seen over here the collapse of my humanistic religion. It cannot stand up against the tides of human pressure. A man must have some standing-ground in the Eternal amid the shifting sands of a semi-pagan world. . . . Above all modern civilization stands the type of life revealed in the New Testament, rebuking the world and offering the only power that can save it."[2] The collapse of humanistic religion in the experience of this typical young liberal foreshadowed a collapse of humanism all along the theological front when the deepening religious needs of the day called for a sturdier theology. Seldom has any prominent system of religious thought gone into such a sudden and complete eclipse as the past two decades have brought to humanism and to the kind of modernism which betrayed Christianity to humanism.

There is a sharp difference between the confused and anemic state of American theology at the end of the first World War and its present robust condition. The poet T. S. Eliot, in explaining a new fervent and active interest in the Church, is said to have remarked, "I began to see that theology is a *masculine* discipline." It

---

[2] J. W. Nixon in *The Christian Century*, February 9, 1944, p. 171.

would be hard to find any group of scientists, philosophers, or other intellectual leaders surpassing the leading theologians of the present day in mental capacity,
breadth of vision, or practical realism. Even American
Protestantism today has leadership of that type. The
Church, therefore, on the whole, has stood its ground
firmly, refusing to be stampeded by the frantic exigen-
cies of the day. It has proclaimed God's righteousness
and God's mercy to a world at war and provided saner
guidance than either the sentimental idealists or the
cynical political realists of secular life could offer. Little
wonder, then, that this time the world is listening with
greater respect to the voice of theologians and that
interest in theology is growing in ever wider circles. In
marked contrast to the formation of the League of Nations, theologians made a distinct contribution to the
thought and work leading to the United Nations. The
preachers most in demand in university chapels are
those who preach Christian doctrine and relate it to
life. The International Council of Religious Education
has turned from its pragmatic techniques to appoint a
Theological Commission to give more solid substance
to its literature. Chaplains place doctrinal theology first
in the list of studies to which they devote themselves
upon returning from the service. Religious interest
among the masses of ordinary people, as well as on the
higher educational levels, has assumed the form of
hunger for definite affirmations of ultimate truth. Significantly enough, General MacArthur in his speech at

the end of the war with Japan said that the solution to our desperate problem of how to build a world which will not destroy itself must be *theological*.

What is the reason for the new vitality of theology? External upheaval, the urgent needs of the day, the failure of other ideologies to satisfy these needs, such factors supply only part of the answer. The fundamental reason is to be found in theology's rediscovery of its own rich resources and its consequent refusal to be any longer a mere parasite on the natural and social sciences. To support this interpretation let me refer to statements by the heads of two institutions which were formerly considered to be strongholds of modernistic theology. Shortly before retiring from the presidency of Union Theological Seminary Dr. Henry Sloane Coffin wrote a book entitled *Religion Yesterday and Today*.[3] In it he portrays vividly the difference between the two theological scenes we have presented. He points out that during the times when the world and the Church seem to have the same faith the Church freely assimilates contemporary secular thought and thus adulterates and weakens its own spiritual force. But today the line separating Christian from pagan is sharp, and the Church is driven back upon its own heritage. The Church lives by the revelation which has been given once and for all in the crucified and risen Christ and transmitted to the individual Christian through the Scriptures and the Church. The Christian has no fel-

---

[3] Nashville: Cokesbury Press, 1940. See pp. 108, 171.

lowship with God except through the Christ of the Gospel vital in the Church. The same emphasis is contained in an essay entitled "Christianity Refinding Itself" by Dr. Ernest C. Colwell, president of the University of Chicago. During his own student days, says Dr. Colwell, the key word in religious discussion was the word "social." The Gospel was the Social Gospel. Church leaders were intolerant of doctrinal abstractions and demanded immediate practical programs for making good on the promises given to the young men sleeping in Flanders fields. "Traditional" was a term of deepest reproach, as was the word "theologian." A hybrid discipline, "philosophy of religion," supplied a more respectable title. Little wonder that few self-respecting students would be seen, even asleep, in a class in theology. The dogmas taught to religious leaders were secular dogmas borrowed from the sciences and philosophy. In the last two decades, however, strong currents in religious thinking have moved away from this position. They all move in the direction of positive theology, of distinctively Christian thinking. "The Church," says Dr. Colwell, "is returning to itself. There is new insistence upon the value of the data and criteria which the experience of the historic Christian community itself furnishes."[4]

The Church's recovery of its own past is expressed in the very titles of such recent works as *The Vitality of*

---

[4] *Religion and the Present Crisis,* ed. John Knox (Chicago: University of Chicago Press, 1942), p. 5.

Christian Tradition, a symposium edited by Dr. George F. Thomas, and *The Thrill of Tradition,* Dr. James Moffatt's last book. Other evidences of the same trend are to be found in new compendia of the thought of Augustine, of Calvin, and of Luther; the vitality of the study of church history, giving rise to such impressive volumes as those of Latourette; the vogue of liturgical movements and interest in correct worship even among denominations with entirely nonliturgical backgrounds; and the founding of vigorous new theological journals with a churchly point of view. Outstanding among the latter are *Christendom,* the organ of the ecumenical movement, and *Theology Today,* dedicated explicitly to the application of the theology of the Reformation to the life of today. In the words of Dr. John A. Mackay, editor of *Theology Today,* "Never must the Church sponsor a blanched, eviscerated, spineless statement of confessional theology. It must give birth in this revolutionary transition time to a full-blooded, loyally biblical, unashamedly ecumenical, and strongly vertebrate system of Christian belief."[5] Current theology is vital in so far as it has become that kind of theology.

II. THE BASIC DIRECTION

What is the basic direction of contemporary theology? This is our second question. The answer has already been partly anticipated. There has been a sharp turn to the right, in the direction of positive historic

---

[5] Editorial in *Theology Today,* April, 1945, p. 5.

Christianity. Tension still exists between the theology thus oriented and a speculative rootless liberalism with an inordinate passion for contemporaneity. There are still those who expect a Whitehead or a Dewey to furnish them religious ideas, while modernists of the older type trim Christianity to conform to the thought-patterns of a James, a Royce, or a Bowne. In some quarters, as among the Baptists and the Disciples of Christ, the old modernist-fundamentalist controversy still smolders. Nor are the humanists altogether extinct, as their journal *The Humanist* shows. But the battle line is now being sharply drawn between historic Christianity and a radical liberalism which veers toward an out-and-out naturalism.

To gain a better understanding of the main trend and to supplement the oversimplified contrast of the two theological scenes given above, let us try to sketch briefly the course of theological development in America during the past quarter of a century. While the first World War was a rude jolt to moralistic and evolutionary optimism, yet, under President Wilson's idealistic leadership, it became a spiritual crusade, a war to end all wars, a war to make the world safe for democracy. American churchmen did not at first share the cultural despair which prevailed in Europe and found expression in the philosophy of Spengler and the theology of Barth. Not even the collapse of Wilson's program with America's repudiation of the League of Nations could kill the social optimism of American progressives.   It now took the form of pacifism, with the Sermon on the Mount as its code and the methods of Gandhi as its strategy. Prominent religious leaders, such as Fosdick and others pilloried in Abrams' *Preachers Present Arms,* repented of their blindness and vowed never again to put Christ into uniform. The Social Gospel and its theological confederate, humanism, were still powerful forces in the twenties. Impatient with the existing order, many religious "progressives" turned toward political radicalism. Sherwood Eddy and Bromley Oxnam were Socialists, while bolder spirits like Harry F. Ward allied Christianity with Russian Communism. The time for a "Christian revolution" was presumed to be at hand, and the American theological front was under a constant barrage of books supposedly carrying the needed dynamite. The depression which began in 1929 vindicated the prophets of social reform, and yet it was this same economic catastrophe which, more than anything else, put an end to the dominance of extravagantly social religion by destroying the optimistic mood upon which it rested. The sense of disillusionment and frustration which replaced that mood paved the way for an appreciation of the more realistic appraisal of man and his possibilities afforded by orthodox Christianity. This new sober and chastened temper was strengthened by the world-wide discomfiture of democracy and the whole inexorable march of events which led to the outbreak of the second World War.

Meanwhile in Europe, ravaged by one war and

careening toward another, the liberal theology resting
upon foundations laid by Schleiermacher and Ritschl
had fallen into utter ruin. Impelled by a sense of over-
hanging crisis, the Church had been driven from alliances with secular thought to seek safety behind the
bulwarks of its own time-tested fundamentals. This was
the dominant trend in all the major branches of the
Church, Roman, Lutheran, and Reformed. Among the
Roman Catholics the revival of Scholasticism, height-
ened by the tercentenary of the canonization of Thomas
Aquinas in 1923, was in full swing. Corresponding to it
in the Lutheran countries was a powerful Luther-renaissance enlisting the leading theologians of Germany
and Scandinavia. From Reformed circles emerged the
mighty prophet of neo-Calvinism, Karl Barth, perhaps
the most influential of all contemporary theologians.

The influence of all three movements has seeped
through, in increasing measure, during the past two
decades into an American theology seeking a new and
more positively Christian orientation. The neo-Scholastic leaders, Gilson and Maritain, found their way into
our greatest universities, and their doctrines found an
exceedingly cordial welcome not only among Roman
Catholics and Anglo-Catholics but even in former fast-
nesses of humanism. At the University of Chicago this
type of thought, sponsored by Chancellor Hutchins, has
led to a drastic revision of educational policy and a
violent break with Deweian pragmatism. At Chicago
we see the curious spectacle of a neo-Scholastic Jew,

Mortimer Adler, leading Protestant students to the feet of Thomas Aquinas. Rebuking the disunity and superficiality of modern society, fighting both naturalism on the one hand and anti-intellectualism on the other, and promising a rational synthesis of faith and intelligence to be applied to corporate as well as individual life, the new Scholasticism makes a powerful appeal to many who have lost their underpinnings. It is not only a revival of medievalism, but a revival which takes account of modern scientific thought. In its idealization of the Middle Ages it has received valuable help from the Harvard sociologist Sorokin, keen diagnostician of the ills of contemporary culture.

Leaving the new Luther-research for later consideration, we must now focus attention upon the movement to which, more than to any other, must be given the credit for turning American theology to the right, namely, the neo-Calvinism of Karl Barth and his many followers. It was to Barth that Americans began to listen already in the early twenties as to the voice of one crying in the wilderness of a corrupt culture, denouncing the false gods of science and philosophy, proclaiming the transcendent sovereignty of the one true God, demanding obedience to His revelation and calling theology to a ministry of His Word. Barth's sermons and popular lectures, in English translation, were eagerly read by ministers of various denominations, and his dogmatic writings, such as *The Doctrine of the Word of God,* showed that theology could be written from a scriptural and churchly point of view with a breadth of scholarship and depth of insight unexcelled by any other approach. Thus Barth became the theological *Fuehrer* of Protestantism, and the dialectical theology which he represented was here called simply Barthianism.

What the widening circle of Barth's listeners has heard is in substance this. Let the world, condemned and under the power of evil, be silent as God speaks. Human science has been weighed and found wanting. It can never yield the absolute values which we seek. There is an unbridgeable gulf between time and eternity, between the world and God. When God speaks, His Word issues from a realm of absoluteness, infinitude, holiness, perfection. When man speaks, his word reveals relativity, limitation, imperfection, sin. The two worlds are thoroughly and qualitatively different. Any human attempt to join them is futile. The finite is not capable of the infinite. We can speak about God only in negative terms. And yet those who are not satisfied with platitudes and complacencies, those who have tried to drink from the empty cups of science and philosophy, thirst burningly for a living God. Here precisely is man's "existential crisis." He cannot get along without God but he has no way of establishing contact with God. This crisis is solved only by revelation from God. Our life and God's life are two parallel lines which can never meet naturally. They can meet only by means of the new line of supernatural revelation drawn from the higher plane and meeting perpendicularly the lower plane. Such a meeting point we have in Christ. But Christ means nothing to one whose religious thinking is still merely intellectual or traditional. Sinful man must face with his whole being the holy majesty of God. Only thus can the "He" attitude toward God become the "Thou" attitude of true Christianity.

Without entering into intricacies and changing emphases of the Barthian system, let us acknowledge that the Swiss theologian has done more than any other individual to strengthen the position of positive Christian theology in our generation. He has exposed the spuriousness of naturalistic and humanistic substitutes for the Christian faith. He has given revelation a genuine content, enabling faith to draw upon its own original taproot, and placed the absoluteness of Christianity upon a strong foundation. Barth's fundamental message has the authoritativeness, the depth and the sincerity of the apostolic *kerygma*. It couples an enlightened biblical scholarship with a profound insight into the spiritual content and living function of the Bible instead of quibbling about the peripheral matters of letter and form. In its devotion to the Word and to the central truths of orthodox Christianity it seems to have retained the virtues of fundamentalism while rejecting its vices. It is not concerned with defending a set of beliefs but with transmitting truth that is at once objectively divine and forever breaking into the human world as a living force.

But there are also elements of weakness in Barthianism which cannot be overlooked. It cannot explain the
experience of faith. It makes such a sharp cleavage between God and man that it fails to show how it is possible for the two thoroughly different beings to come
together at all. Barth insists that man through sin has
lost his point of contact with God, that the divine image
in man has been completely destroyed. Yet when and
because God speaks to him, man hears, and although
he has no capacity to recognize the Word as the Word
of God, he nevertheless does so. Brunner, originally a
Barthian, solves this difficulty by parting company with
Barth and holding with the Lutherans that man's spiritual nature, even in its sin-perverted state, still affords a
point of contact with God. The only valid conclusion
from Barth's premises is unmitigated predestination according to which God quite arbitrarily gives faith only
to whom He chooses. A second difficulty in Barthianism,
the cosmic counterpart of the preceding one, is its extreme transcendentalism which leads consistently to
deism. Barth finds no traces of God either in the world
or in reason and disagrees even with Calvin himself in
denying any general revelation or natural theology.
This position fails not only to give adequate recognition
to divine immanence but it also encounters insuperable
difficulties in trying to explain the incarnation, the
union of the divine and the human in Christ. The only
recourse is to acknowledge an impenetrable mystery
expressible only in paradoxes. Finally, Barthianism is

stronger as a criticism of a Church which has been untrue to its mission than as a constructive proclamation and program of the Church. It has been more effective in disarming man of his own weapons than in helping him to put on the full armor of God. Barth correctly reproves man's sinful disregard of the distance between him and God, but lacks the strong Lutheran emphasis on the grace which eliminates the distance, creates the fellowship of faith, and empowers for action.

Emil Brunner, who began his theological career as a disciple of Barth but has developed into a creative independent thinker whose emphases coincide more fully with those of Luther and of classical Protestantism, has come to wield an influence as extensive as Barth's. His popular books, such as *The Divine-Human Encounter* and *Justice and the Social Order,* have brought the insights of the dialectical theology within the reach of the average preacher, while his comprehensive systematic works, *The Mediator, The Divine Imperative, Man in Revolt,* and *Revelation and Reason* are the finest modern treatises in these fields available in English. Having enjoyed first-hand contacts with such movements as the Social Gospel, the Oxford Group, and the Ecumenical Movement, and being thoroughly at home with theological developments in both Europe and America, Brunner has sought to bridge the gulf between the Gospel and present-day culture. His question has been: How can I, a minister of the Gospel, interpret this precious gift to the thinking men of my generation to whom Christ has become a stranger? When Brunner accepted a teaching position at Princeton a few years ago, his coming was expected to have the same significance for American theology as the coming of Whitehead to Harvard had for American philosophy. Brunner soon returned to Switzerland, however, but another of the dialectical theologians, Paul Tillich, has become a permanent fixture at Union Theological Seminary and has literally brought a new depth-perspective into our theology. Reinhold Niebuhr is the outstanding example of what has happened to American thinking under the influence of the type of thinking represented by Barth, Brunner, and Tillich. Niebuhr has not ceased to be an American with an intense interest in social problems, but he has a depth and a realism drawn from the original Christian Gospel and sadly lacking in the Social Gospel.

Few prominent American theologians are out-and-out Barthians. E. G. Homrighausen, G. W. Richards, and Edwin Lewis may perhaps be properly so classified. But, on the other hand, few of our theologians have escaped the Barthian influence. President Mackay and his associates at Princeton Theological Seminary typify the creative use Americans are making of this influence. How widely and deeply Barth's teachings have become imbedded in American minds, whether they acknowledge it or not, was strikingly revealed by the "How My Mind Has Changed" series of articles appearing in *The Christian Century* in 1939. To most of the thirty-two representative American religious thinkers the thirties were a decade of rediscovery. Edwin Lewis acknowledges his debt to Barth for a rediscovery of the meaning of revelation. Barth helped Walter M. Horton rediscover Augustinian theology. Georgia Harkness discovered that the Church has foundations which are not of this world and that the "Body of Christ" is more than a time-honored phrase. John C. Bennett rediscovered the permanent value of the Christian view of man, and that rekindled an interest in theology which had almost been swamped by ethics. Halford Luccock and Ernest F. Tittle confessed to a swing from moralistic to God-centered preaching. Even Henry Nelson Wieman, outstanding exponent of an immanental naturalistic theology, had been led to reexamine Paul and as a consequence had had some blind spots removed with regard to sin and grace, the living Christ, the Church, and the otherness of God. Robert L. Calhoun's thinking had undergone a veritable "revolution" from a philosophical to a truly theological orientation.

No less important than its direct contributions has been the function which Barthian theology has served in mediating to us the "existential" philosophy of Sören Kierkegaard, the young and obscure Danish thinker of a hundred years ago, who is today regarded by many as the outstanding intellectual genius of the nineteenth century and the profoundest Christian thinker since Luther. It was from Kierkegaard that Barth learned the absolute qualitative difference between the temporal and the eternal, the distance separating sinful man from God, the inadequacy of intellectual as well as of institutional Christianity, and the importance of the existential moment in which man, stripped of all his pretenses, has to submit to divine cross-examination. It was Kierkegaard who engineered that Copernican revolution in religious thought by which we give up our futile and sinful attempt to focus the searchlight of our reason upon God and instead allow our whole life to be examined in the light of divine revelation. To Kierkegaard, Christian truth is not man's inquisitiveness about God, leading to understanding of some sort; it is God himself taking hold of man, changing him and giving him a new life in responsibility and obedience. Christianity is not a matter of belief or opinion, nor does it rest on the facts of science or the speculations of philosophy. It is a matter of faith, and faith is "existential communication," something deeply subjective, unique and incommunicable, something that happens to a man when he encounters God. That man, separated from God by sin, should have such an encounter is itself a miracle, comparable and related to the central miracle which Christianity proclaims, namely, incarnation, the fact that eternity has entered time, God has become man, walked on this earth, and died on a cross planted on one of its hills.

A Christianity which started out with a "gospel" announcing this magnificent paradox has gradually in the course of the centuries changed into a Christendom, an organized body of nominal believers content with a second-hand knowledge about Christ in the place of first-hand faith. Christendom has gained a spurious intellectual respectability at the price of giving up the Gospel which alone gives it a right to exist. The Church must stop putting out a "cheap edition" of what it means to be a Christian. It must be honest enough to admit that the divinity of Christ cannot be proved by general rational or historical evidence, but He is God only to those who are willing to follow and obey Him in faith. Kierkegaard dedicated himself to the task of restoring the specifically Christian point of view, of being a missionary calling Christians to be Christian.

Just as Nietzsche in announcing "God is dead" was right in the sense that God had ceased to be real to the majority of his contemporaries, so Kierkegaard was undoubtedly right in insisting that vast numbers of Christians had actually stopped being Christian. Both Kierkegaard and Nietzsche, correctly reading the "signs of the times," sensed the impending struggle between a supernaturally oriented Christianity and the modern mind which gives its primary credence to natural science. Nietzsche took his stand with naturalism and became the spiritual ancestor of twentieth-century Nazism which glorified power and rode roughshod over Christian standards. Kierkegaard was just as decisively a Christian. That is why his thought is so timely and valuable to Christian theology today, now that the conflict he foresaw has come to a head.

Most Americans had never heard of Kierkegaard before being introduced to him by Barth. Now the Kierkegaard-renaissance is rolling forward, on its own merits, arresting the attention of all serious students of religion. Soon all the writings of Kierkegaard will be available in English translation, and a useful anthology of his thought has recently appeared. Another existential Christian thinker of the past who is coming to his own in America today is Pascal, who has found a competent interpreter in Emile Cailliet.

III. THE CENTRAL THEMES

We have studied in some of its ramifications the basic trend in current American theology. Our next angle of approach is to examine some of the specific doctrines upon which attention is being focused in contemporary theological discussion. In the *Christian Century* series of articles to which reference has already been made, H. C. Phillips says that he finds himself preaching on more and more central themes. Such is also the case with the theologians proper. The central issues have become the live issues. In the immediate past theological discussion revolved around such themes as the relation between science and religion, the relation between biblical criticism and the authority of the Bible, and the logical validity of religious experience. Today attention has shifted from such penultimates to such concrete ultimates as God, Man, Christ, and the Church, the Body of Christ.

God. Considering first the concept of God, the present trend is from immanence to transcendence, away from conceiving God as an aspect of nature or of society, toward acknowledging Him as the "wholly other" and sovereign Lord whose will is ultimate reality and who reveals himself in concrete historical events. Characteristic American thought on God was represented in the older generation by Lyman Abbott and in ours by Henry Nelson Wieman. In his *Theology of an Evolutionist* Abbott attacked all ideas of "creation by manufacture" and advocated the view that God is a vitalizing principle within the cosmic process, "dwelling within the universe, and shaping it from within, much as the human spirit dwells within the human body and forms and controls it from within." In the same spirit Wieman makes various attempts to express the meaning of God. While he holds the exact nature of God to be problematical until scientific method has become further improved, God is an object in man's natural environment, yielding value to human living when the right adjustment is made. God is "that Something upon which human life is most dependent for its security, welfare, and increasing abundance,"[6] a Something to be defined in terms of an impersonal process of interaction or integration. Wieman is bent upon discovering a

[6.] *Religious Experience and Scientific Method* (New York: Macmillan, 1927), p. 9.

"minimum God" on which all can agree and discovering such a God in the observable behavior of nature. Like its historical forebear, primitive magic, this "scientific" approach seeks to manipulate the divine for the achievement of its own values, without giving God himself any voice as to the conditions upon which He may choose to reveal himself. As late as 1938, in a book written jointly by Wieman and Horton, entitled *The Growth of Religion* and heralded as the foundation of an indigenous American theology free from foreign alliances, the authors define God as "the growth of living connections of value in the universe." This view, however, grounded in evolutionary immanentism and patterned on the "concrescence" of Whitehead and the "holism" of Smuts, does not seem to satisfy even the authors themselves. The following year finds Wieman pondering on the possible otherness of God. Wieman is a good example of a rootless and restless liberal who has sought in vain to find anchorage in any branch of historic Christianity. And Horton, whose intimate acquaintance with, and acute sensitiveness to, current theological tendencies the world over make him a peculiarly valuable weather vane of winds of doctrine, writes three years later: "Immanentism is distinctly a handicap to Christian thought in the present age, which has witnessed the outburst of colossal forces of evil and destruction throughout the globe. A God to whom we can look with trust and hope today must be a God who transcends these destructive forces, towers over them commandingly, has his seat of authority so high above them that their heaven-storming assaults dash themselves in vain against his lofty throne."[7]

But such a God cannot be derived from an analysis of the external universe. He is the God of Christian faith. This "God of the Christians," as Pascal[8] saw, the God who makes men "inwardly sensible of their misery and His infinite mercy," is not the "God of the philosophers" "who is simply the author of geometrical truths and the order of the elements." "He is found only by the paths taught in the Gospel," only in Jesus Christ. When present-day theologians have sought to read Christian theism into "the order of the elements" as expounded by Whitehead, Einstein, and Dewey, they have received well-merited rebukes from these philosophers themselves. How far short of the God of Christian faith even the philosophers deliberately friendly to it fall, when they follow faithfully their own methods of empirical observation and rational reflection, is illustrated by the God of A. C. Garnett, who is only the altruistic good will in man; that of Charles Hartshorne, who is absolute in some respects and seeking perfection in others; and that of E. S. Brightman, whose will is struggling to subdue a recalcitrant element within His own nature. No theology can be Christian unless it abandons definitely the idea of an unknown Something

---

[7] W. M. Horton, "Theology in the Present Crisis: God," *Alumni Review*, Presbyterian Theological Seminary, Chicago, July, 1941, p. 48.

[8] *Pensées* (Havet ed.; 1922), pp. 78, 79, 389.

to which we must somehow make an adjustment, the end-result of some logical or moral process, and concentrates upon the God who entered into human history in His Son and confronts us in His Word. Vital theology flourishes today where theologians have seen the limited value of scientific and philosophical analyses of the sources and meaning of the general concept of God and follow the method of Christocentric existentialism inherent in the Christian faith itself.

Man. With the trend toward a more Christian view of God and a more adequately God-centered theology has come the trend toward a more Christian estimate of man. We are beginning to realize that neither classical Greek philosophy nor modern science with all its psychological and anthropological techniques has given us the true measure of man. What they have missed is the dimension of depth in human nature, the insight into the tremendous potentialities for good and for evil, contained in the Christian doctrine of man as created in the image of God, corrupted by sin, and restored by Christ. The outstanding recent work in this field is of course Reinhold Niebuhr's two-volume *Nature and Destiny of Man,* the most impressive American contribution to the Gifford Lectures since William James' *Varieties of Religious Experience* nearly a half-century ago. Some competent critics go so far as to claim that this work will mark a new epoch in American theology. Niebuhr proceeds from the Kierkegaardian starting point that man does not know himself truly except as he knows himself confronted by God. In that confrontation he becomes aware both of his spiritual stature and of his evil, of his God-likeness and of his creatureliness, of his freedom and of his finiteness. Original sin is a perennial human situation resulting from his egocentric unwillingness to acknowledge his dependence, to accept his finiteness, to admit his insecurity. The limitations themselves are not sin, but the refusal to accept them is. Since man cannot avoid lust for power, pride, and self-deification and yet has no way to overcome frustration, he is caught in a terrible dilemma of grandeur and misery and lives in an inward state of restless anxiety. In the justification of sinful man, Niebuhr stresses Luther's principle of *"simul iustus et peccator,"* that even the justified believer is both righteous and sinful at the same time. He is righteous because he has exchanged his sin for Christ's righteousness, but he is such only in principle. In fact his sinful nature remains. In his analysis of culture, Niebuhr repudiates the evolutionary view of the redemptive character of history. History only unfolds, in increasing measure, the depths of good and of evil and culminates, as Christian eschatology correctly sees, in the struggle between Christ and Antichrist.

Niebuhr's diagnosis of man's sinful predicament is profound and scriptural, and he makes skillful use of the tension of sin and grace to throw light on the historical life of man. But while he has caught much of the spirit of classical Protestantism, his basic outlook, like

Barth's, continues to be more prophetic than evangelical. He fails to grasp the dynamic which grace contains for the renewal of life, both individual and corporate. The contrast between being justified in principle and in fact is misleading, for it overlooks the constructive fact that justification is the basis of sanctification. These strictures, however, do not impair the value of Niebuhr's great work as marking a definite turn toward positive Christian truth about man. It is a theological watershed which cannot be ignored by anyone who seeks to trace our human problems to their roots.

Christ. When theology begins to re-examine its concepts of God and of man, it cannot escape a fresh study of Christ. The reason is stated clearly by Horton in the Introduction of his *Our Eternal Contemporary:* "We have discussed the nature of God and the nature of man; next in order, unless we dodge it, is the question of the right relationship between God and man. This is the Christological problem, for Christ is the Christian answer to the age-old problem of the right relationship between God and man."[9] Unfortunately in much of our current religious literature the question is dodged; for example, in Joseph Gray's *The Postwar Strategy of Religion* the Church is admonished to proclaim "the great historic affirmations of the faith which constitute the gospel," but the author gives only three such affirmations: the reality of a supernatural world, the existence of God, and the immortality of man. There is no

_____
[9] New York: Harper's, 1942, p. xviii.

Christological or soteriological affirmation. Yet there are signs of a deepening recognition that only Christ can build the kind of new men and women that are needed for the construction of a new world order. The incarnation and the atonement are being studied afresh in the light of new exegetical and historical research. There is a growing appreciation that the faith of the ancient Church, as expressed in the formula of Chalcedon and the idea of ransom, is far richer than the oversimplified moralism of our prewar days. Much of our contemporary thought on Christ is still shallow discussion of the religion of Jesus rather than genuine theology of Christ the Mediator and Redeemer. But the constructive trend is unmistakable. Horton's book, mentioned above, reveals the influence of the Lutheran Christologists Heim and Aulén and points definitely to the right. Other recent works showing the same trend are William Adams Brown's *How to Think of Christ,* William Manson's *Jesus the Messiah,* John W. Bowman's *The Intention of Jesus,* F. W. Dillistone's *The Significance of the Cross,* and Henry W. Clark's *The Cross and the Eternal Order.* Dr. Clark's portrayal of the cosmic significance of Christ is especially impressive and shows affinities with the thought not only of Aulén but also of Althaus and of Kuenneth. Here is the theology behind the idea popularized by Stanley Jones: life has been so constructed that only by commitment to Christ will it work. The most inspiring guide, however, that our generation has to fruitful thinking about

Christ is Karl Heim, who has crowned a distinguished theological career with a series of profound works in Christology.

The Church. The fourth of the central themes of contemporary theology is the Church. After an age of individualism in which a great philosopher could define religion as "what a man does with his own solitariness," theologians even in America have suddenly awakened to the fact that Christianity is not primarily a body of ideas or a code of regulations or a set of principles, but a fellowship, a community of life in Christ. To some, as to Georgia Harkness and Charles Clayton Morrison, this discovery came with the force of a new revelation. The latter was so dazed by the brilliance of the insight that he thought no Protestant had ever thought of it before and charged Luther with having introduced the "Protestant heresy" of individualism. He did not know that what he regarded as Protestantism was only a sectarian perversion of it and that, in rediscovering the Gospel, Luther had also rediscovered the nature of the Church as the fellowship of the redeemed in which we are "Christs one to another." It is no mere coincidence that the Ecumenical Movement was set in motion by a Lutheran archbishop, Söderblom, and that the Swedish theologians of the present day, heirs of his rich legacy, are contributing some of the profoundest insights we have into the nature of the Church Universal. In this field we can learn much also from the representatives of two other branches of the Church, the Anglican and the Greek Orthodox, both of which have cherished and cultivated a meaningful concept of the Church as a supernatural reality, the mystical Body of Christ, the sacramental and organic togetherness of the faithful in their Lord. At all events, ecumenicity is the key word for today's Christianity, and all living doctrine proceeds from that viewpoint. It would be impossible to over-estimate the impetus, the fresh depth, and the broader horizons religious thought in America has received through the ecumenical conferences at Oxford, Edinburgh, Madras, and Amsterdam. We cannot begin here even to sketch the vast literature to which they have given birth nor to appraise the importance of the new vision of a world-church with a world-mission in such a day as the present. Suffice it to say that as the result of these new emphases the discussions of the Church's role in the postwar world are marked by less starry-eyed optimism and unevangelical activism and by more sober realism and greater determination to carry out the slogan of Oxford: Let the Church be the Church.

Our survey of the contemporary theological scene indicates not only the prevalent trends but also the positive normative emphases which should govern the-ological thinking and doctrinal preaching in our day. Already in choosing from a more or less chaotic post-war situation the trends worthy to be discussed and thus excluding many others, we have been compelled to make value-judgments. We have said nothing, for example, about the various currents of apocalypticism and millenarianism which prolonged war always sets in motion. The basic prerequisites of a living theology still appear to me to be the four which I set forth in assuming my theological professorship fourteen years ago.[10] First, theology must be guided by its objective reference. This means that the theology of the Church Universal must be a theology based on revelation, a Christ-centered and Bible-centered theology. True theology cannot rest on the kind of speculation to which the existence and nature of God is still an open question. It is called to give expression to the concrete faith of the Christian fellowship, not to exploit controversial metaphysical principles. With true insight the basic article of the World Council of Churches demands faith in Jesus Christ as Saviour and God. Second, theology must spring from its historical roots. The Church itself is essential to the Gospel, an integral part of revelation, the sphere of God's activity. One who is not at home in the Church deserves no hearing as spokesman for the faith of the Church. A Christian theologian does not spin the web of his thought out of his private theorizing; he draws his data from a continuity of revelation which spans the centuries and which the Spirit of God keeps vital in the Church. But in the light of history, the claim of any one branch of the organized Church to be exclusively the Body of Christ must be repudiated. When the Roman Church, for example, makes such a

---

[10.] "Some Prerequisites of a Living Theology," *Lutheran Church Quarterly*, April, 1934, pp. 105-24.

claim, it must be shown to be only a large sect. Third, theology must speak the language of the living. A doctrinal statement, even a confessional one, as the *Formula of Concord* wisely expresses it, is a witness to the truth rather than its judge. Christian truth is dynamic, and its greatest foe is static intellectualism, encased in set formulae by which the hands of the dead keep their grip on the helm. Living theology speaks to men "in their condition"; it does not say the same thing to a generation driven by fear as to a generation ruled by pride. Fourth, theology must serve the living Church. This means that theological truth is never an end in itself but must issue in a life of obedience and service in the Christian fellowship. As Dr. John A. Mackay has recently put it, "It is the final task of theology to provide an instrument of Christian advance in every sphere of life and thought."[11] Theology must validate her claim to be the queen of the sciences by providing the ultimate meaning and objective for all the sciences and arts, for all education and philosophy. Not only must theology speak God's truth to all mankind but also produce Christians who in every sphere of life can outthink and outlive their generation, because they are the exponents of nothing less than God's eternal purpose in our Lord Jesus Christ.

IV. LUTHERAN THEOLOGY IN THE NEW DAY

Against such a background and in the face of such

[11] *Op. cit.,* p. 10.

demands what is the message of *Lutheran* theology?
The succeeding chapters will attempt to outline the
answer. In making the transition from the setting of
our study to its center, let us recall that along with the
revival of Thomas Aquinas in Roman Catholic neo-
Scholasticism and the resurgence of Calvin in Barthianism, our century has witnessed also a Luther-renaissance. It finds magnificent expression in the complete
critical edition of Luther's works, the Weimar edition,
begun in 1883 and now approaching its goal of 104
volumes. Besides the general interest in the recovery of
the religious heritage of the past, which we have observed, various specific factors have contributed to the
new interest in Luther. First, the use of the exact methods of modern historical science, originally applied to
a study of the Reformation by Ranke a century ago,
has been remarkably rewarding. Primary sources which
have lain buried for centuries have been brought to
light. The discoveries began in 1877 when a student's
copy of Luther's pre-reformatory *Commentary on Galatians* was found in a second-hand bookshop in Cologne.
Within the following decade some hitherto unknown
sermons of the Reformer were found in Zwickau, as
well as seven books which Luther studied as a monk
and provided with his own marginal notes. Then the
important *Commentary on the Psalms* came to light in
Dresden. In 1899 the archives of the Vatican Library
yielded early commentaries on Romans and Hebrews.
The crowning discovery came in 1905 when Ficker

found in Berlin Luther's own original manuscript of his 1515-16 *Lectures on Romans*. Marvelous new light is thus shed especially on the young Luther, and his fundamental theological convictions are seen to ante-date the beginning of the Reformation. Added incen-tive to the study of Luther has been furnished by the necessity of answering misrepresentations by the Roman Catholic writers Denifle and Grisar and mis-understandings by Protestant scholars such as Troeltsch. To list the men who have contributed to this study would be to name almost every prominent theologian in the Lutheran countries of Europe. The pioneer in the research was Karl Holl, who clearly established, as over against Troeltsch, that Luther was not a medieval thinker but an original religious genius who rediscov-ered the Gospel for the modern world.

It was the misfortune of the Reformation that its great living truths received their systematic formulation in an age when the basic thought-forms were supplied by a decadent Aristotelian Scholasticism. Consequently the new wine of the rediscovered Gospel was poured into the old skins of static intellectualism. With Luther it was not so. Like Pascal and Kierkegaard after him, he was one of the greatest "existential" thinkers of all history. He did not cast his thinking in the Aristotelian mold. He did not make the mistake of dealing with God as a physicist deals with matter, i.e., as with an imper-sonal entity. The definition of God given in the Augs-burg Confession, "There is one divine essence which is

called and is God," is not his handwriting. In Luther's
language, "God has no divinity where there is not
faith."[12] He stood *"coram Deo,"* in the presence of God,
never merely speculating or talking *about* Him but responding *to* Him with his whole being as person to
person. Nor did he petrify God's Word into a system
of abstract concepts. The Word was God himself speaking to him personally and reaching beyond his intellect
into the innermost depths of his conscience. The method
of living Lutheranism is therefore to go beyond the dry
and ponderous systems of our orthodox Scholasticism
to Luther himself for guidance and inspiration and to
face the problems of our day in the spirit which motivated him. It is to follow his example in courageously
breaking free from lifeless forms of traditional churchly
speech and practice and to yield absolute loyalty to the
living Christ alone.

So far the Luther-renaissance has only begun to
make its impact upon American thought. Interest in
Luther's own writings has grown, to be sure, and American scholars like Preserved Smith, McGiffert, and Reu
have carried on Luther study. More recently, Boehmer's
biographical studies of Luther, Nygrén's masterful
analysis of Christian love, the Christology of Aulén and
of Heim, and the eschatology of Althaus have definitely
left their mark upon American theologians. Barth and
Brunner, too, always drawing heavily upon Luther, have

[12.] *Weimar Ausgabe* of *Luther's Works* (hereafter designated WA),
XL, I, 360.

helped to keep him in the field of awareness. Pauck at Chicago, Piper at Princeton, and Bainton at Yale have made broad creative applications of their intimate knowledge of the new Luther research. But American Lutheran theology itself is still largely oriented in the seventeenth century, and, adhering to the traditional scholastic methods, continues to busy itself with old distinctions and abstractions quite remote from the present theological battlefield. Unlike European Lutheranism it has tended to develop a self-satisfied and anathematizing mentality and to join forces with an utterly un-Lutheran fundamentalism. No theology can be genuinely vital unless it develops sound self-criticism in the light of that living Gospel which no doctrinal system of any age can adequately express to another age, and Lutheranism can nowhere find a more severe or more constructive critic in this respect than Martin Luther himself. As the Church goes forward to meet the needs and the opportunities of a new day, it is to be hoped that the rediscovered dynamic Luther may obtain a hearing among Lutherans in America as well as among American Christians in general. To further this hope the present series of studies aims to set forth in the setting of the contemporary scene and in the light of the Luther-renaissance the three key-principles of Lutheranism: justification by faith, the authority of the Word of God, and the universal priest-hood of believers.

CHAPTER II

JUSTIFICATION BY FAITH
AND THE MAN OF TODAY

To PAUL and to Luther, as well as to the evangelical Christianity which has followed in the paths they blazed, "justification by faith" is pivotal among all Christian truths, the article by which the Church stands or falls. The right of Protestant Christianity to exist rests upon its proclamation of the Gospel epitomized in this doctrine. If the business of the Church is to minister to man's natural religiosity, to discover and to reinforce the forces of good in human nature, to teach people to live on as high a moral plane as they can, assuring them that God will help them and reward them, and to erect a powerful and well-organized ecclesiastical empire to gain prestige and influence for carrying out these aims, then it is unnecessary duplication and waste to maintain a Protestant system seeking in vain to rival Roman Catholicism. But if with Luther and Kierkegaard we acknowledge a valid distinction between true Christianity and organized Christendom, if Christianity brings new life from above to the spiritually dead, not merely moral medicine to the spiritually ill, if this new life is the gift of God's free unconditioned grace to everyone who in the commitment of "faith" entrusts himself, person to person, to the God who seeks him in judgment and mercy, and if the function of the Church is to confront men, both within and without Christendom, with a Gospel which mediates such first-hand contacts with God, then not only does the Church of the Reformation have a permanent God-given mission but the Gospel it lives by must be rediscovered as a vital force for each generation.

Our generation has had difficulty in appreciating the meaning of justification by faith, partly because of the proud secularism of the modern temper, partly because of the neglect, the distortion, or the unnecessarily pedantic and abstract formulation of the doctrine itself in the proclamation of the Church. The most recent historical developments, however, especially the discovery of tremendous power by which mankind can bring about in a single day its own complete destruction, have tended to break the crust of godless self-sufficiency. Conscious of the moral bankruptcy of secularized education, disillusioned as to the messianic pretensions of science, appalled by the threatened doom of our whole civilization, generals and statesmen, as well as scientists and educators, have turned to the Church with a plea strangely reminiscent of the man in ancient Philippi who cried from the verge of suicide, "What must I do to be saved?" Even though this newly awakened sense of the need for spiritual guidance may be concerned only with temporal security rather than with fitness to face God, at least basic evangelical theology is today receiving a hearing such as it has not had for many generations, and man's extremity may still be God's opportunity. Hence the answer which the Church gives to the modern cry of distress should be as direct and unequivocal as Paul's was to the Philippian jailer: "Believe in the Lord Jesus, and you will be saved." The doctrine of justification by faith derives its importance from the fact that it sets forth the meaning of that answer. If the change in the modern mood toward greater receptivity is matched by a corresponding change in theological thought and expression toward vital clarity, this doctrine may once more be shown to be God's own answer to the supreme need of men as in the days of the Apostles and of the Reformers. To this end, let us examine the doctrine: (1) in its scriptural and historical background, and (2) in its peculiar relevance to the present day.

I. SCRIPTURAL AND HISTORICAL BACKGROUND

On what ground can man, cut off from God by his sin and guilt, be acceptable to God and enter into a living personal fellowship with Him? The answer stems from the heart of the Gospel, Jesus' love for sinners. To the pious devotees of Old Testament religion it was self-evident, as it is to most religious people today, that God looks with favor only upon those who have done their best to obey His Law. They were outraged, therefore, when Jesus by precept and by example flouted such a fundamental principle. This man, they complained, although He claims to speak in the name of God, "receives sinners and eats with them." But He would reply, "I came not to call the righteous, but sinners." On one occasion He proceeded to tell them an astounding story about a lost son, comparing God to a father who lavishes his affection upon a moral derelict whose only claim to consideration was his utter helplessness and need. In another illustration He drew a sharp contrast between a Pharisee, a devout keeper of the Law, and a publican, self-condemned before the Law and appealing only to God's mercy. Jesus concluded: "This man (the publican) went down to his house justified rather than the other." Here the term "justified" is used in the precise theological sense of being acceptable to God, and the way of justification is shown to be the way of faith and grace as distinguished from the way of the Law. The divine love which freely pours itself upon the undeserving shines in its full glory from the Cross, where the innocent Sufferer prays for His malefactors and with His pierced hand opens the door to paradise to a dying criminal. After the disciples had experienced the reality of the resurrection of their Lord, reflection upon the whole drama of the Cross could not fail to disclose new depths of meaning in the words He had spoken earlier: "The Son of Man came to give his life as a ransom for many" and "My blood . . . poured out for many for the forgiveness of sins."

Such was the source from which Paul developed his doctrine of justification, expressed in such majestic assertions as these: "Since all have sinned and fall short of the glory of God, they are justified by his grace as a gift, through the redemption which is in Christ Jesus, whom God put forward as an expiation by his blood, to be received by faith" (Rom. 3:23-25) and "God shows his love for us in that while we were yet sinners Christ died for us. Since, therefore, we are now justified by his blood, much more shall we be saved by him from the wrath of God" (Rom. 5:8-9). Understood in its rich fullness, including its mystical, ethical, and eschatological, not only its forensic aspects, this doctrine is clearly as central in the theology of Paul as in that of Luther. It is true that modern scholars from Fichte to Schweitzer have questioned this centrality, but their criticisms pertain properly only to one-sided and abstract formulations of the doctrine. In his *Mysticism of the Apostle Paul* Schweitzer claims that Paul's central doctrine is the mystical "being in Christ" and that this is based on Jesus' death as such and His resurrection as such, not on any forensic considerations of infraction of law and the need of vicarious sacrifice. Justification by faith thus becomes only a secondary fragment of Paul's mystical religion, developed casually in a more or less accidental controversy and serving only the expedient purpose of disposing of the legalists.

Schweitzer goes on to trace the alleged weakness of the practical ethics of Lutheranism to a wrong exegesis of Paul's teaching. Unlike the Apostle's invigorating mysticism, justification by faith is held to be quietistic and unable to create ethical dynamic.

The importance of Paul's Christ-centered mysticism must not be minimized. The expression "to be in Christ" occurs no fewer than 165 times in his writings. The centrality of justification, however, rests on the solid fact that no aspect of his experience can be understood except in the light of his Jewish background. To Paul, a Pharisee of the Pharisees, zealous for the heritage of the fathers, the way of salvation was the way of the Law. The Law was the standard which God uses in measuring man and determining his fate. But that way led to an impasse. How different was Paul's experience from that of the psalmist who declared: "The law of the Lord is perfect, restoring the soul" (Ps. 19:7). To Paul, too, the Law is holy and righteous, but it leads only to despair. The Law demands complete fulfillment, an impossible task for sinful man. What a terrific struggle a true Pharisee must have undergone before he could confess: the Law is not the way of salvation! It brought to Paul only a sense of guilt. Moreover, to him the Law was not a mere impersonal code but God's will, His demand, His revelation. In the light of this revelation the zealous Pharisee, with all his religiosity, discovered his basic maladjustment to God. His soul-agony thus took this form: How can I stand before God in the eschatological day of judgment when now in my conscience before God's Law I stand under wrath and judgment? And how can I meditate on God's Law day and night when that Law only condemns me and goads me to despair? It was this inwardly crushed man, unaware as yet of the depth of his own disillusionment, who had an encounter with the living Lord Christ on the Damascus road. What happened there is a mystical secret between Paul and his Lord, but the consequences of the encounter were tremendous. Paul found a new and true way of salvation. It is the way of *pure undeserved grace*. God, not man, is the active subject in the work of redemption. God was in Christ reconciling the world with Himself. Christ is the end of the Law, for He is God's new standard. Saving righteousness is not the result of a struggle to do the works of the Law. It is God's own free gift to us. And the proper response to a gift is not strain and effort but joyful acceptance. But to accept God's grace in faith does not mean to find a way to avoid God's judgment-throne. It means to find a way to meet judgment. Because God's standard of judgment is His own grace, not the Law, He justifies the ungodly. He therefore accepts with favor the sinner who entrusts himself to the divine redeeming purpose, even though he stands condemned by the Law. Justification is essentially the forgiveness of sins. The Gospel which proclaims it is the word of acquittal spoken to the sinner and declaring him to be righteous on the basis of what Christ has done. But it is also the power of God which creates a new filial relation to God and provides access to all the riches of His grace. Gospel, grace, and faith are correlative terms describing God's sovereign love in thus justifying a sinner. They are the antitheses of Law, works, and merit.

This new way of salvation came to Paul as such a revolutionary experience that he had to say: I died to the Law and became a new man "in Christ." There is nothing casual or secondary about it. If Paul had not discovered this way of righteousness, he would have discovered nothing. It is true that the Apostle proceeds to present his message in terms of dramatic metaphors rather than logical concepts. But whether he describes man as a slave who has been purchased to be free, or an enemy who has become reconciled to enjoy peace with God, or a debtor whose debt has been paid, or a branch cut off but engrafted to nobler stock, or the dead coming to life, he is in every case concerned with God's new way of dealing with man—grace, instead of the Law. To single out one of these metaphors, the acquittal of one who stands accused before the Law, and to erect an entire theology upon it, as Luther did, may appear at first to be arbitrary. But if any one of Paul's figures of speech can stand the whole weight of his thought, this is the one, for it most clearly expresses the fundamental contrast between Saul and Paul, the Law and the Gospel.

It would be a grave mistake, however, to separate justification by faith from the new life it bestows. For in forgiving our sins God gives us not just a formal pardon but His own living presence. Christ's death for sinners makes possible the forgiveness of sins, but His resurrection makes possible a living contact with the power of a new risen life. The new life is participation through the Spirit in the living Christ present in the Church. Paul's doctrine of justifying grace is too rich to be expressed by any one word, forensic, ethical, or mystical. There is an objective forensic side: *Christus pro nobis*. There is also a subjective ethical and mystical side: *Christus in nobis*. Underneath is the basic tension between the present world and the world to come. Christ has already triumphed over the demonic powers dominating the present evil age, but they will not be fully overthrown until His second coming. The new world to come has already begun with Christ's resurrection and the believer lives at the same time in both aeons. Already he is justified through faith and achieves victories through the power of his Lord's resurrection, but his final justification is eschatological. It is with reference to the final judgment at the Lord's second coming that Paul is led to say: "I know nothing against myself; yet am I not hereby justified: but he that judgeth me is the Lord" (I Cor. 4:4). He realizes the serious possibility of ultimately becoming a castaway if he allows the powers of this evil age to obtain mastery in his own life. The Christian thus lives in a constant tension between "pistis" and "elpis," confident possession and hope, the imperfect and the perfect, the now and the then. We hope to be saved from the wrath to come, but already there is no condemnation for those who are "in Christ." He who has begun the good work will fulfill it in the day of Christ Jesus. We possess all things in Christ, but we yearn for His coming. Now we see darkly in a mirror, then face to face. To the end Paul remains "the chief of sinners" who despairs of finding any way out of his sinful predicament, but it is the confident despair of a sinner whose fate is in the hands of the God who in His mercy justifies the godless.

The Pauline doctrine found its most adequate theological interpreter fifteen centuries later in Martin Luther. But we cannot appreciate the Reformer's rediscovery of the grace that justifies a sinner unless we understand how it had become intellectualized, moralized, and ritualized in the Roman Catholic Middle Ages. Very early in ancient Catholicism justifying grace becomes limited and channelized through identification with baptismal grace, the maintenance of which is thought to require merits and good works. In the teaching of Augustine the original Pauline emphasis makes its last appearance before it is completely submerged in Scholasticism. Augustine identified grace with the Holy Spirit and insisted that without His activity the will of man, totally enslaved by sin, is incapable of doing anything toward salvation. The Spirit operates as "prevenient grace" in creating a new heart in man, and as "co-operating grace" in every good work of man. The Augustinian stress on predestination is a particularly strong expression of the primacy and sovereignty of the divine redeeming purpose, as over against man's efforts to save himself. While in its central trend Augustine's thought on justification is thus a bridge between Paul and Luther, it contains also elements of Neoplatonic mysticism and ecclesiastical sacramentarianism which fitted into characteristic medieval interpretations.

To the Roman theologians the Reformation came as a surprise very difficult to meet because they had no uniform concept of grace or justification. In fact Peter Lombard's *Sentences*, widely used text in dogmatics, does not even treat justification as a specific doctrine. On the whole, grace was regarded as a super-physical power poured from above into man's nature to bring about a "habitus" or quality of the soul. To Duns Scotus it was a moral, to Thomas Aquinas a metaphysical, power. Augustine's identification of grace with the Holy Spirit the Scholastics could not accept, for the Spirit is a person and therefore cannot be impersonally infused. The mystics spoke of grace either as participation by man in the nature of God or as the incarnation of God in the soul of man. A closer fidelity to the Pauline doctrine is found in the Nominalists Occam and Biel who taught that grace is divine favor by which God sees fit for Christ's sake to forgive the sins of the believer, but grace lost its essential redemptive meaning through excessive stress on divine sovereignty.

The dominant theologian of the Middle Ages was Thomas Aquinas. From his master Albertus Magnus he had inherited the idea that grace is divine benevolence which aids man's upward striving, filling in the deficiencies and intensifying the spiritual powers. But Thomas sought to synthesize the various elements of Catholicism by means of a logical dialectic. As against the Franciscans he stressed the sovereignty of grace but he also sought to adjust it to the idea of merit. He blended Augustine's "sola gratia" with Aristotle's "prime mover." There is a preparatory grace which is solely divine activity in which man does not co-operate. But the grace which justifies is an infused power poured into the ground of the soul to create a spiritual disposition to take the place of the old sinful disposition. Justification involves four steps: (1) the infusion of grace, (2) the redirection of the will toward God so that faith and love become blended, (3) the setting of the will against sin, and (4) the remission of sins. Grace remains something impersonal, standing between man and God, rather than a direct relation of fellowship. It was lost through the Fall but through the sacraments it is infused as a supplement to man's natural state.

The Council of Trent, after a long debate, rejected thoroughly the Pauline and Lutheran conception of *imputed* grace and subscribed to Thomas' idea of *infused* grace. Man is therefore justified not by grace alone but by faith, hope, and love, the virtues generated by the grace poured into his heart. This grace is mediated by the seven sacraments which attend the Christian from baptism to extreme unction. Justification has four causes: (1) the efficient cause, God, (2) the meritorious cause, Christ, (3) the formal cause, the sacraments, and (4) the final cause, the glory of God and the salvation of the soul. In a word, justifying grace is an impersonal metaphysical power, it operates through a ritualistic agency, it involves co-operation between God and man, and it results in a psychological change whereby man ceases to be a sinner and actually becomes a saint. Thus Roman Catholicism in its final form destroys Paul's and Luther's paradox by which a Christian has a sinful and a saintly self at the same time. The saint is altogether a saint, no longer a sinner.

So influential is this view, and so congenial to reason, that not even Karl Holl, the great pioneer in Luther research, could see clearly how radical was Luther's departure from it. In explaining Luther's *Lectures on Romans* Holl presents this interpretation of Luther's view. A righteous God must hate sin and therefore He can justify only those in whom He has chosen to begin and finish His work. Holl attaches great importance to Luther's illustration of a physician who pronounces a convalescent patient to be already well. Thus a time-transcending God, to whom the beginning and the end are the same, can pronounce the *iustificandi* (those that are to be justified) to be *iustificati* (those that are justified). When He forgives a sinner, it is an indication that He will actually by a gradual process make him righteous. The first to attack Holl's interpretation was Wilhelm Walther, followed by a host of other theologians. The case against Holl may be summarized as follows: (1) Such passages as the one dealing with the physician and the patient do not have basic doctrinal significance but are used by Luther in a pastoral sense to encourage Christians of weak faith. Moreover, Luther there describes not justification but the daily sanctification of the believer already living by grace. (2) Holl is not free from the natural moralism of the Scholastics and of Kant and Ritschl. He therefore fails to do justice to the unconditioned nature of grace. That God should justify the godless is a paradox which can be explained only on the basis of God himself, not by anything He sees in us.[1]

Luther's position can be understood best by taking right seriously his expression "simul iustus et peccator," righteous and sinner at the same time. Sormunen[2] has analyzed the content of this term into four basic thoughts: (1) Monergism of grace. God is the only active agent in justification. All human free will and co-operation are ruled out. Unless grace is allowed to do all that is to be done, justification cannot be sure. On any other ground man robs God of His glory and him-

---

[1] Professor Uuras Saarnivaara, in a hitherto unpublished dissertation, agrees with Holl's interpretation of the *Lectures on Romans* but dates the "tower experience," through which Luther discovered the true meaning of justification, after the Lectures, thus solving the entire controversy by distinguishing between Luther's earlier and later view.

[2] Eino Sormunen, *Jumalan Armo (die Gnade Gottes)*, (Helsinki: 1934), II, 112-13, 304-5. This work by Finland's pioneer Luther scholar has been an invaluable aid in the present study, specifically in the exposition of the thought of Paul and of Luther on grace.

self of assurance. (2) Original sin is not only the occasion for sin, as Aquinas had taught, but it involves personal guilt. Man's natural inclination to sin and repugnance toward God are damnable. Concupiscence is *my* concupiscence. The moment I think I have overcome concupiscence I fall into the original Satanic sin of pride. (3) Man as a *whole* is a sinner. I cannot draw a psychological or metaphysical distinction between the soul and the body, assigning sin only to the latter. The whole man is in a wrong relation to God. In Luther's words, "Totus homo caro," the whole man is flesh. (4) Justification for sinful man is procured by "Christus pro nobis," who, when appropriated by faith, becomes "Christus in nobis." Because Christ died for us God declares us to be righteous, but the declaration is accompanied by the gift of His renewing Spirit. Again the whole man is involved: "Totus homo spiritus."

The doctrine of the continued sinfulness of the saints placed Luther outside the Roman Catholic church. If the pope had not excommunicated him, he would have been remiss in his professional duty, because Luther cut the very heart out of Roman Catholicism. To the Roman church Christ is the source of grace, but grace itself is a metaphysical medicine which trickles down from Christ via the Church, the hierarchy, and the sacraments, to make the sin-sick soul well. To Luther grace is a personal relation, a direct experience of judgment and forgiveness. Sin is more than sickness. It is guilt. It causes a gulf which cannot be bridged from our side. God himself must bridge the gulf and renew the broken personal relation. Man not only commits sins. He is and remains a sinner. But through the Word of the Gospel he faces the God whose glory it is to forgive sins. Man's own works never attain to any merit before God, and he therefore remains humble and dependent, but by faith he lives, day by day and moment by moment, on God's grace.

The "simul iustus et peccator" idea is specifically developed in Luther's *Lectures on Romans*. Before the Gospel comes to us, he tells us, we are "totus caro," in complete carnal peace and indifference. The Gospel is the good news of grace, but its effect is to bring about a conflict between flesh and spirit, the old man and the new man. Since "flesh" stands for our whole self-centered nature, we cannot get rid of ourselves and fulfill the Law of God. The fact that we are not satisfied with being sinners saved by grace alone but seek to gain merit by fulfilling the Law shows our inalienable natural pride. When we do accept God's grace we are freed from the Law and from God's wrath and judgment. The believer is *iustus*, as distinguished from *peccator*, *spiritus* as distinguished from *caro*. But since the believer is also a man, a constant tension remains. Luther agrees with Augustine that the seventh chapter of Romans with its dramatic conflict between spirit and flesh describes Paul *after*, not *before*, he became a Christian. How else could the Apostle say that with the spiritual man he agrees to God's law? Nor does a carnal man cry out: "Wretched man that I am, who will deliver me?" While Luther has much to say about the new life wrought by the Spirit, he never endorses perfectionism. It is because we cannot become sinless that the Law has a permanent function in disciplining the old man in us. Our righteousness is imputed, not earned, and it is ours only through Christ.

In the large *Commentary on Galatians* the relation between grace and the Law receives a most systematic exposition. According to Roman Catholic doctrine, man must prepare himself for grace by turning away from the natural and seeking the spiritual. When he has reached the point when he hates sin and freely loves God, grace is infused and man is justified. But Luther discovered with Paul that man can never reach that point. The Law is God's will as it concerns me personally. It calls me into His presence. The function of Moses is to lead us out of our tents to hear God speak. The Law has accomplished its work when like the children of Israel we cry out: "We shall die! Let not the Lord speak!" Terrified conscience should drive us to Christ who calls the heavy-laden and promises rest. The Law is thus God's "opus alienum" performing a useful negative task preparatory to grace, which is God's "opus proprium." But Moses should not be allowed to torture awakened consciences. He must be chased to the light-hearted sinners. Evil conscience is conscience terrified by the Law. Good conscience is conscience freed from fear by the grace of God. Without a terrified conscience there is no pacified conscience. But the devil seeks always to pervert the Law from its proper use and make it a way of salvation, which it can never be. The Law in its perverted devil-allied use is one of the powers of destruction over which Christ triumphs. Christ is not a lawgiver but a forgiver. But since the believing sinner is still a sinner, the Law continues to have a permanent function as regards the flesh. The believer thus lives in an unresolved tension between the terrible reality of the demands of the Law, the wrath of God and judgment, on the one side, and the assurance that there is no condemnation for those who are in Christ, on the other.

"Simul iustus et peccator" appears in various other writings of Luther. In *The Bondage of the Will* he points out that the Gospel ministers to our weakness while the Law appeals to our strength, to our reason and free will. By means of the Law and free will men can work "civil righteousness" which is right and proper in its own sphere. It becomes downright dangerous, however, when men confuse it with divine justice and seek thereby to earn their salvation before God. Reason seeks man-made ways of salvation and free will seeks to carry them out. Reason thus allies itself with the Law and makes it the principle of self-sufficiency. Free will is the old man, the natural man, in action. It commits the "double sin" of failing to fulfill the demands of God's Law and of despising God's grace. Law becomes perverted in this way into an instrument by which

Satan leads men to his own false way of salvation eventuating either in false certainty and pride or in despair and doubt. With deep spiritual insight Luther tracks sin not to man's lower nature but to his highest and best nature, his reason and will.

In the last analysis "simul iustus et peccator" means that Christ and Satan are in conflict over man. It is thus an amazingly rich principle dealing not only with justification itself but also furnishing the clue to Luther's Christology, soteriology, and eschatology. Through the Law and its application to evil conscience Luther brings the cosmic struggle between Christ and Satan into the heart of the individual. When Satan is in the ascendant, I have a terrified conscience. When faith sees Christ as the conqueror of Satan, I have a peaceful conscience. It is my constant experience as a believer to be both damned and pardoned. I am a sinner, but in faith I can say to Christ, "Thou, Lord Christ, art my sin and I am Thy righteousness." Where there is forgiveness of sins, there is life and salvation, there is heaven. Hell, too, is to be understood in terms of conscience. Christ suffered hell in His own conscience to the point of temptation to blasphemy when he cried: "My God, why hast thou forsaken me?" There is no depth of agony or temptation where Christ has not descended before us and whence He cannot save us. The victorious Christ himself is present in faith. Even such a doctrine as "communicatio idiomatum" ceases to be an abstraction and serves the interests of living faith. It signifies: Christ is at once the exalted Lord and yet accessible to faith. He has conquered death and Satan and He can conquer them in me. The real presence of Christ in the sacraments issues from the same root. There is a definite reference to "simul iustus et peccator" in the explanation of the permanent significance of baptism as a daily return of the penitent sinner to a childlike receptivity of regenerative grace. The doctrine of predestination itself is stripped of heartless despotism and becomes the final demonstration of God's sovereign purpose to save sinners.

The development of the concept of justification after Luther can here be sketched only in the barest outline. Luther, like Paul, had foreseen the difficulties attending the preaching of the doctrine. "The forgiveness of sins ought to make you glad," he had once said, and then had quickly added, "This is the chief Christian doctrine, and nevertheless a most dangerous thing to preach."[3] The pitfalls soon made their appearance. Just as Jesus and Paul had been accused of undermining morals, so Luther was attacked on this ground by both Roman Catholics and sectarian fanatics. Little wonder that Melanchthon, whose Aristotelian and humanistic leanings made him particularly sensitive on this issue, sought to heighten the sense of moral responsibility by toning down the emphasis on "grace alone" and admitting human co-operation into the saving process. The ensuing theological battle was officially won by

---

[3] WA XXVII, 378, 9.

Melanchthon's opponents, who, following Luther, excluded entirely the activity of man's will from justification and made God the only active agent. However correct the doctrinal position thus assumed, the practical result was to lead to a danger of another kind. The whole matter came to be removed from the realm of experience into the realm of purely conceptual analysis. Justification became a purely forensic affair, dealing not with man at all but only with the relation between man and God. It was said to take place not in the human heart but in the judgment hall of God. Much was written about the way in which sinful man in general becomes justified before God but little about the way in which this or that individual can come to a personal assurance of justification. The general answer, of course, was that he must believe the word of justifying grace. But how? As Karl Holl[4] puts it, shall he read the story of the prodigal son or of the repentant thief and then say to himself: "Now I am justified"? Shall he do this when conscience accuses him or must he endure the pangs of conscience a while? Or must he wait to hear the comforting word from the lips of another? These questions, furthermore, presuppose an awakened conscience. What happens when an effortless salvation as a formal intellectual scheme is preached to men in whom conscience is asleep and moral earnestness is lacking? The result is a static uniformity which sub-

---

[4] *Die Rechtfertigungslehre im Licht der Geschichte der Protestantismus* (Tuebingen, 1922), 2 aufl.

scribes to the form of true religion but lacks its life-changing power. Such was the general tendency of Orthodoxy. Since justification was not discussed in terms of personal experience, evangelistic fervor burned low and attempts to penetrate beyond the standardized concepts of pure doctrine to the emotional springs of religious life were characterized as fanaticism. Violent opposition to Calvinistic predestination and vehement affirmation of the written Word as the sole vehicle of revelation tended moreover toward the idea of a God who does not concern Himself directly with the affairs of individual persons but in a more or less deistic fashion views objectively the working of His creative and redemptive processes in the world.

The inevitable reaction to Orthodoxy came in the form of Pietism. The movement initiated by Spener and Francke, and extending its influence not only throughout the Lutheran world but far beyond it through such men as Zinzendorf and Wesley, is essentially a return to the original emphasis of the Reformation upon heart-felt personal religion. Justification is to be experienced in terms of individual regeneration. While it provided a much-needed and vital corrective, Pietism in running its course uniformly manifested an overemphasis upon man and his emotional states. It thus led to the setting up of arbitrary and artificial marks of regeneration and to consequent legalism. The differences between Orthodoxy and Pietism, however, must not be exaggerated. In the perspective of subsequent history we can see their inner interdependence. Orthodoxy needs Pietism to escape petrification into theoretical external objectivism, and Pietism needs Orthodoxy to escape falling into morbid emotional subjectivism. Both held to the age-old Christian presuppositions of justification: that the righteous will of a personal God is life's basic reality, that man by violating this will has become enmeshed in sin, that restoration of a right relation to God is only through the redeeming work of Christ. The dawn of the "age of reason" in the eighteenth century, which challenged these fundamentals themselves, brought about a radically new orientation of the whole religious problem. Freed from ancient intellectual as well as political and ecclesiastical tyrannies, and finding a new guide in the rising scientific spirit which accepted as true only what is mathematically demonstrable, the men of the Enlightenment entertained the idea of God at best only as an intellectual hypothesis to account for the order and reasonableness of the universe. To enter into direct relations with Him in terms of personal responsibility was foreign to the spirit of the age, and the idea of finding relief for distressed conscience from a unique revelation of a redemptive process mediated by a chosen people such as the Jews was laughed out of court. Man insisted upon his natural right to happiness and assigned to ethics and religion the function of ennobling and satisfying the quest for happiness. Instead of holding himself accountable to God for his sin, man called God to account for those things in the universe which thwarted his happiness. The problem of evil thus pushed aside the problem of sin, and God's justification of man had to give way to theodicy, man's effort to justify God.

It is obvious that in describing the eighteenth century we have already touched on something quite up-to-date. Our American democracy in particular, born out of the spirit of the eighteenth century and carrying in the Declaration of Independence and the Constitution classical expressions of that spirit, still clearly shows its birthmarks. But much of our thinking on God and man is still more directly rooted in the intervening nineteenth century which remains to be briefly characterized. To Immanuel Kant must be given the credit for having outthought the eighteenth century and having set up the problems with which the nineteenth was to grapple. He vindicates his title, "the philosopher of Protestantism," with his clear rediscovery of Luther's insight that the ground where God and man meet is conscience and that there man is confronted with an inescapable and unconditioned imperative. Had Kant gone on from there to develop his further insight that in following the voice of duty man discovers in himself a "radical evil," he would have been a true Lutheran indeed. But he was too deeply intrenched in the pride of the Enlightenment to beg for grace, and instead of grounding morality upon religion, he grounded religion upon morality, found his key-principle in an autonomous moral will, and reduced God to the role of rewarding human virtue. Ritschlian moralism and modern liberalism with their stress on the intrinsic worth of moral personality are legatees of the Kantian heritage. At all events, the moral and spiritual elements in man and the supernatural element in the universe, to which they point, had once more obtained a roothold in an enlightened modern man's view of life. This position was further strengthened in post-Kantian idealism. Hegel's God is not, like that of the Deists, an obsolescent point of reference on the ultimate fringe of things. He is the dynamic agency who is at work in history and gives it meaning. Schleiermacher discovers God's energizing activity within the depths of his own consciousness. In an important work dealing specifically with *Justification and Reconciliation* Ritschl seeks to give a moral synthesis of the historical and the psychological points of view. These impressive systems and their numerous progeny in various interblending forms of historicism, moralism, and psychologism undoubtedly served as bulwarks preventing spiritual values from being submerged by the rising tide of man's godless self-glorification in a century in which natural science became the unquestioned ruler of the intellectual realm and received due obeisance from such courtiers as evolutionary naturalism and positivistic humanism. The religious philosophers of the nineteenth century, however, failed utterly in their efforts to bring man and God together. They sought to relate the finite spirit to the infinite and failed to see that man's basic difficulty lies not in his finitude but in his sin. Since they forgot to ask whether sinful man is capable or worthy even of aspiring into fellowship with God, they had no genuine appreciation of the Christian doctrine of mediatorship. As Fichte expressed it: A Christian needs no other tie to God beside the fact that in Him we already live and move and have our being; every man by being born a man is already in the Kingdom of God, for only on that condition is he a man.[5] Such an initial assumption can lead to no reality beyond itself and issues only in an endless effort to reaffirm itself. The one nineteenth-century thinker of first magnitude who refused to be stampeded by the spirit of the time and saw clearly the chasm separating the sinner from God was Kierkegaard. It is to be noted also that the evangelistic and missionary movements of the century which kept Christianity vital among the masses of the people were motivated not by the new forms of thought but by the old-fashioned preaching of justification through grace. Among the Lutherans such preaching received powerful impetus already in the first quarter of the century from a new interest in the Reformation occasioned by the tercentenary of its beginning. Its principal forms of expression were a more determined confessionalism and the experiential theology of the Erlangen school representing a revival of Pietism. The stage was thus set for the Luther-renaissance of the twentieth century, which,

---

[5] "Grundzuege des gegenwaertigen Zeitalters," *Saemtliche Werke,* VII, 104.

together with the resurgence of Calvinism, has brought justification once more into the foreground of theology.

II. RELEVANCE TO THE PRESENT DAY

Compared with the florid self-satisfied optimism of four or five decades ago, the mood of the present day is much more congenial to the Christian Gospel of sin and grace. The dreams of a utopia which man was to build for himself without any help from God have turned into horrible nightmares. After two long and costly wars supposedly won by the forces battling for freedom and democracy, these goals are farther from the grasp of most nations than before. The war to make the world safe for democracy led to the rise of ruthless dictators, and the war to overthrow Nazi tyranny strengthened and emboldened Communist tyranny. Those seeking to deal with the present menace are impaled on the horns of a dilemma: either prepare for a new war, more devastating than ever, if not utterly destructive, or else follow a Munich-like policy of appeasement for the sake of peace at any price, a policy which has already proved its impotence in the ultimate prevention of war. Add to this picture the new weapon of atomic energy by which man is said to be able to destroy not only the planet he inhabits but the entire solar system, and it is not difficult to understand the sense of futility and precariousness which pervades the present outlook. The significant fact is that while formerly the fear of perdition haunted chiefly the uneducated masses, now the most frightened people are the most educated. The most urgent preachers of the new hell-fire are the most advanced scientists and the most realistic statesmen. Few believe that any idealistic talk of "justice" will long hold in check the naked force upon which international relations now rest. The chief ground for optimism appears to be that the exhaustion caused by the war just ended will prolong the period of cheating between two periods of fighting, as peace has sometimes been defined.

Is the doctrine of justification by faith to be preached to such an age as a "deus ex machina," a miraculous divine intervention which will clear up the mess we have made and lay our fears to rest? God forbid. The forces of faith are not at man's disposal simply because he wishes they were. Hagar's thirst, as Karl Heim expresses it, does not cause a spring to bubble up in the desert. The point of view to which justification is diametrically opposite is wishful thinking. It does not cater to man's desire but appeals to his conscience. It calls him from his pursuit of happiness to face his responsibility before God. It is not concerned with the way in which either an individual man or the race as a whole can prolong their physical existence but only with the way in which men can straighten out their relation to God. Since it centers around the eternal nature of God, it would be vindicated rather than invalidated, should man choose the path of godless self-destruction. The Gospel of justification knows no way of circumventing the cemetery. Both believers and unbelievers, both individuals and cultures, must die sooner or later. Nor is justification by faith anything but a strange and irrelevant doctrine wherever men, relying on their own wisdom, strength, and goodness, are confident that they know how to work out their problems, or where they believe that by organizing or reorganizing intelligently the outward conditions of life, its economic, political, and social relations, they can insure their security. So long as a man can give himself fully to his work and his home, has health and the respect of his fellows, cultivates enough intellectual, esthetic, and cultural interests to enjoy self-respect, makes friends and a fair amount of money, belongs to congenial organizations, secular and religious, in a word, so long as the whole versatile business of living has the air of a going concern, such talk as sin and justification is sheer nonsense. Those who are well have no need of a physician. All these values, however, turn hollow when the man has been compelled to face in the solitude of his conscience not others but his own innermost self and has discovered there an incurable anxiety, an aching emptiness where God ought to be. When man has thus become his own biggest problem, when he recognizes his need of God but honestly owns up to a sense of guilt which cuts him off from God, then the doctrine begins to make sense. And when man refuses to drug the awakened conscience to sleep and is not content to worship God from a distance, but, come what may, submits without reservations to cross-examination by God himself, then justification by faith opens the door to a triumphant personal fellowship with God, which neither life nor death can dissolve.

The meaning of justification can be summed up in simple present-day terms in the form of four propositions: (1) It shows how God and man come together on a basis whereby God is God and man is man. (2) The ground where God meets man is conscience. (3) The person-to-person relation with God thus established is the source of regenerative power. (4) The right relation to God results in the right relation to fellow-man.

1. *God is God,* first of all, and *man is man.* Every profound theology of justification, whether of Paul or Augustine, Luther or Calvin, proceeds from a radically theocentric starting point. In the words of Paul Althaus, "the Gospel is first and last the word that God is God."[6] It is grounded not upon man's striving for security, affection, or worth, but upon the revelation of God's sovereign will to save. Luther's rediscovery of the Gospel, as Holl was the first to point out, had an intimate connection with the first commandment. When God says, "I am the Lord thy God," He reveals His will to be my God, and what more can Christ do than make God *my* God? To take this commandment seriously, then, is to believe the Gospel which invites me "just as I am" into personal fellowship with God. I am a sinner, I must confess, but the God who wills to have fellow-

---

[6] *Theologische Aufsaetze* (Guetersloh, 1935), II, 125.

ship with me can be trusted to provide the forgiveness which will make the fellowship possible. Luther is thus led to interpret Psalm 130:4, "There is forgiveness with thee that thou mayest be feared" as meaning: "there is forgiveness with thee that thou mayest remain God."[7] It is God's sovereign will to save us by grace alone. As Althaus observes, this is not because man is a sinner but because the sinner is a man, and God's way with man is the way of grace. Because He is God He wills to be Creator and Giver, to create out of nothing, to do all the giving. But man in his insolent stupidity, says Luther, is not satisfied with receiving God's gifts. He wants to give something back to God, "to do something big." He thus commits the blasphemy of robbing God of His divinity, of reducing God to the passive role of viewing man's achievements. Justifying faith which lays the foundation for a sound relation between man and God is at bottom simply obedience to God's will to be God. It rolls down the curtain on the unholy farce of man trying to play God and lets the Giver of every good and perfect gift act His own part.

Man plays the part of God so poorly because, unlike the divine love "which seeketh not its own," man, as Luther says, "cannot but seek his own and love himself above all, which is the sum of all sins."[8] Man's sinfulness does not consist essentially in his failure to control

---

[7] WA XL, III, 360.

[8] *Vorlesung ueber den Roemerbrief 1515-1516*, ed. J. Ficker (Leipzig, 1930), II, 75, 8. This work hereafter referred to as Ficker.

his lower nature from acts of overt indecency. Such control is established with relative ease by ordinary worldly etiquette. To be a saint is much more than to be a gentleman. But not even the saintliest of saints is free from the craving for power nor from the danger of pride. Even in his worship of God man thinks naturally of his own blessedness as the chief end and thus renders only corrupt reverence. No matter how spiritual a man may become, he never wins complete freedom from such natural determinants as the one implied in the adage, "Self-preservation is nature's first law." So complex is human nature and so intermingled in every act are higher and lower motivations that we cannot advance beyond the word: "If we say we have no sin, we deceive ourselves" (I John 1:8). In the very act of claiming sinlessness we exhibit the most Satanic of sins, spiritual pride. The unconscious driving forces which we hide even from ourselves because they are so different from the reasons we consciously ascribe to our conduct may be all the more dangerous because they are hidden. Modern psychologists have pointed out that no individual is completely integrated around any single pattern, good or bad. Every man, according to Jung, has within him a genius, a criminal, and a saint. Or to use Kunkel's example, a burglar is not 100 per cent successful in his trade because he is only 70 per cent burglar and 30 per cent decent man and good father. Literary men who have cultivated a keen observation of human nature have arrived at the same result. The gripping realism of Somerset Maugham's stories can be understood in the light of this excerpt from his own credo: "How scornful we are when we catch someone out telling a lie; but who can say that he has never told not one, but a hundred? We are shocked when we discover that great men are weak and petty, dishonest or selfish, sexually vicious, vain, or intemperate; and many people think it disgraceful to disclose to the public its heroes' failings. There is not much to choose between men. They are all a hotchpotch of greatness and little-ness, of virtue and vice, of nobility and baseness. Some have more strength of character, or more opportunity, and so in one direction or another give their instincts freer play, but potentially they are all the same."[9]

Reflection along this line helps us to appreciate the soundness of Luther's insight: "simul iustus et pecca-tor," saint and sinner at the same time. But we must also bear in mind the Reformer's insistence that the whole man is involved both in the sinfulness and in the saintliness. "Totus homo caro, totus homo spiritus." Man is not partly sinful and partly saintly, as though there were something in him which no longer needed forgiving grace. Contrary to the superficial view of sanctification held in common by Roman Catholicism and the holiness sects of Protestantism, human nature neither originally possesses nor later achieves a sound spiritual area which is unaffected by sin, for sinful ego-centricity has its seat in our highest spiritual powers,

---

[9] *The Summing Up.*

reason and will. The whole man in his Satanic revolt against God is "flesh"; the whole man in Christ-governed obedience to God is "spirit." In himself he is altogether unacceptable to God; in Christ he is altogether acceptable. That is why justification is solely by the faith which puts all its trust in Christ. And that is why the boundary line separating the saint from the sinner runs its deepest course not between men but between two selves within the same man, the self that trusts in itself and the self that trusts in Christ. In a recent sermon on Peter's denial of his Lord, Reinhold Niebuhr made an illuminating application of this principle. In each of us, as in Peter, are both a loyal self, the Peter of the Garden, and a traitorous self, the Peter of the courtyard. The idealist sees only the former, the cynic the latter, the Christian both. But when we are confronted with God's judgment and love, still another self is born, a truly spiritual penitent self which lives by forgiveness. When evangelical theology affirms that justification is "by faith alone," it calls precisely for this confrontation of sinful man as a whole, with his intermittent braveries and betrayals, by the judging and pardoning God. The saintly or spiritual self thus born never ceases to be a penitent self, for it cannot subsist on its own but only on the grace of forgiveness.

With the acknowledgment that God is God and man is man, justification may be defined as the sovereign and merciful act of God in accepting with favor the sinner who admits his own utter inability to be anything but a sinner and therefore thankfully receives fellowship with God as a totally undeserved gift. The divine activity, the sole causal factor, is grace. The God-awakened receptivity in man, which places him within the divine activity, is faith. When grace is seen to operate through the atoning work of Christ and is contrasted with man's own futile efforts to satisfy the demands of God's justice, then justification may be presented in the forensic terms often used by Paul and the Reformers and formally schematized by traditional orthodoxy. A courtroom scene is presented in which the divine Judge, having found the sinner guilty on the basis of his own actions, nevertheless pronounces him to be innocent because an "alien" righteousness, that of Christ, which he has appropriated in faith, is "imputed" to him. To use a kindred figure of speech, while an examination of the sinner's ledger reveals him to be morally and spiritually bankrupt and deserving of the debtor's prison, he nevertheless turns out to be solvent, since faith has placed to his credit all that Christ has earned. Justification is therefore "propter Christum per fidem," on account of Christ and through faith.

Such a method of presentation has done much to preserve the factual objective character of the Gospel and to guard the purity of its central content, the free grace of God, unconditioned by anything in man. But exclusive dogmatic preoccupation with this form of doctrine has its dangers too. Just as ethical idealism reduces God to be the spectator of human achievement, so forensic orthodoxy, if it stops there, leaves man to be the spectator of a divine drama. In seeking to avoid the spectator-attitude and to keep alive the "existential" character of justification as an actual encounter between man and God, we come to the second of our four propositions.

2. *The ground where God meets man is conscience.* In expressing the matter thus, the word "ground" of course is used figuratively, for conscience is not a place of any kind, nor is it indeed any separate organ or faculty in man. It is rather, as Bishop Ljunggren of Sweden has shown in his penetrating study *Synd och Skuld i Luthers Teologi,* man as a whole viewed as "homo theologicus," seen in the perspective of theology to be a personal being to whom God speaks and who is therefore a responsible "thou" to his Maker.[10] Since man is a sinner, conscience first manifests itself as "evil conscience," the awareness of maladjustment to God. A man becomes aware of God as a person only when he has become aware that his will has crossed God's will. The resulting sense of guilt leads a sensitive conscience to self-examination but it also points to a higher Presence. In responding to that Presence, if man is honest, he will have to confess his incompetence and unworthiness even to address God as one person addresses another. "I have taken upon me to speak to the Lord, which am but dust and ashes" (Gen. 18:27). Who am I to presume that there is any common ground between

---

[10.] Pp. 56 ff.

God and me or to expect that He will pay any attention to me? It is the pure in heart who see God, and my heart is not pure. It is only under these conditions that the Christian Gospel of the God who loves the sinner comes into its own.

> "Thy promise is my only plea,
> With this I venture nigh:
> Thou callest burdened souls to Thee,
> And such, O Lord, am I."

A vital personal relationship between man and God thus comes into existence, but its sole ground and constant pivot is the forgiveness of sins. The believer keeps the "mystery of faith," the experience of the redeeming rendezvous with God, in a "clean" or "good" conscience, the conscience in which Christ is Lord. His life is a constant series of the decisions of faith in which he responds seriously and gratefully to the Word which invites sinners into God's presence. He thus continues to accept life as a gift from the hand of God and to wrest the victory of faith from the forces of unbelief.

This road from the distress of guilt-burdened conscience to the peace of God has been traveled through deep inward struggles by such men as Paul and Luther who have thought out the doctrine of justification. We cannot grasp its true meaning simply as the end-result of a theological analysis without embarking on the same venture of personal faith. Nor is its goal reached, as is commonly supposed, when man has received comfort of conscience and the hope of eternal happiness. Since the contact with God takes place on the ground of conscience, it involves man's whole personality, not just his desire to be comforted and happy. The initial encounter with God is indeed anything but happy, and man's natural desire is to run away and try to forget the whole matter. Nor does justifying grace ever allow a man to use God as a kind of fire-escape from hell. Far from having anything to do with man's own happiness, says Luther, fellowship with God is "to seek the will of God and His glory in all things and to desire nothing for one's self either now or in the future life."[11] A faith which concerns itself principally with the fear of hell and the hope of heaven is still weak and childish. A strong conscience-bound faith affirms the righteousness of God's judgment even if it condemns man to perdition. He whose conscience is thus bound to the will of God is undisturbed by happiness or lack of it, temporal or eternal. But such a resignation of the human will to the divine triumphs over hell itself, for the very willingness to accept, if it is God's will, even eternal separation from God is the final proof of unbreakable will-fellowship with God. Thus the heroic travelers of the road of justifying faith, Augustine and Luther and Calvin, arrive through the depths of the darkest despair at the same triumphant conclusion as Paul: "There is therefore no condemnation to them which are in Christ Jesus. . . . For I am persuaded that neither death nor

[11.] Ficker II, 217, 23.

life, nor angels nor principalities, nor powers, nor things present nor things to come, nor height nor depth, nor any other creature, shall be able to separate us from the love of God which is in Christ Jesus our Lord" (Rom. 8:1, 38-39).

Never was this approach to man's basic problem more urgently relevant than in our day. Now that the thought of "the earth being removed" and "the mountains carried into the midst of the sea" has become something more than a poetic metaphor, the faith "Therefore will not we fear, for the Lord of hosts is with us" needs also to be more than a sentimental vagary or a stereotyped platitude. But God will remain distant and unreal to modern man until his life's journey, like that of Kierkegaard, has passed from the stage of esthetic enjoyment to the stage of ethical earnestness and thence to vital personal Christianity. In spite of the tragedy that has stalked us, the Danish prophet's description of the first stage still fits most of us. Driven by a demonic pursuit of the joy of living, supported only by ourselves, we dance over the abyss as a stone skimmed over the surface of the water "skips lightly for a time, but as soon as it ceases to skip, it instantly sinks down into the depths."[12] The skipping may take the form of work or of play, of strenuous effort or of sensuous indulgence, but it is punctuated by boredom and cynicism and eventuates in enervating despair. How to awaken in a generation with such a life-orientation a

[12.] *Either–Or*, I, 105.

sense of moral responsibility, if only for the sake of avoiding disaster, is recognized today as the problem of highest importance by political and intellectual, as well as religious, leaders. Mr. John Foster Dulles, for example, in a recent speech on "The Atomic Bomb and Moral Law" insisted that the most determined efforts on the part of statesmen to prevent war or to limit its destructiveness by means of international law and organization are doomed to failure, unless what they are doing reflects honestly the moral judgments of the rank and file of the nations. More powerful than atomic energy, he said, is the power of world opinion, but that in turn rests upon the specific attitudes of individual men and women. World problems thus turn out to be personal problems, or, as Kierkegaard would put it, the concrete decisions which you and I make in the actual business of living tie the knot which fastens the thread of thought to the fabric of existence. From the tortuous road of conscience there is therefore no scientific or political short cut to safety. If, however, this point of view of moral earnestness is maintained, in the face of what the Word of God demands, the acknowledgment of personal guilt is inevitable. In the light of an awakened conscience it is sheer escapism for me to blame any other criminal but myself for the condition the world is in. Not only have I been guilty of moral stupidity, impotence, and lethargy in following my own selfish ends while my fellow-men were being engulfed by mortal danger, but my sinful self-will has actively contributed to the sum-total of the world's evil. It is true that a handful of men crazed by the lust of power, defying God and trampling down those who were not of their own kind, precipitated the tragedy. But my conscience affirms the truth of the Word that says, "Thou that judgest doest the same things," there is a potential Hitler in thee. The basic trouble lies in the high-handed and treacherous rebellion of my will against God and my consequent betrayal of my fellow-man. These broken personal relations can be restored only through forgiveness. The road of conscience, if pursued to the end, thus winds up in an impasse from which we must be lifted by the pure grace of God offered by the Gospel of justification.

3. When God is God in all the creative sovereignty of holy love, and man is man in the guilty helplessness of his whole nature, and a genuine meeting between the two takes place on the ground of God-awakened conscience, it follows as a consequence of this contact that conscience is "purged from dead works to serve the living God" (Heb. 9:14). We thus arrive at the third aspect in the meaning of justification: *Man is taken into a personal fellowship with God which is the source of regenerative power*. Here is the central affirmation of the entire Christian message. The Gospel of justifying grace is the life-changing "power of God." Paul uses the boldest of all possible metaphors when he speaks of it as a duplication in human experience of the Easter miracle: we die with Christ and rise with

Him into a newness of life (Romans 6). The forgiveness of sins is never an end in itself. It is the beginning
and ground of a fellowship, a new filial relation to God.
Forgiveness is in fact the only basis for a truly new
beginning, for it not only rectifies the relation to God
with reference to present status and the direction of
future activity, but it also removes the burden of the
irrevocable sins of the past which weigh upon the conscience. If it is astounding that God should have anything to do with us, it is still more astounding that He
can carry out His own purposes in us and through us.
This is because He presents us with no formal pardon
but with His own living and abiding Presence. Faith
not only rests upon the objective fact "Christ died for
us"; it is constantly renewed and energized by the
Christ who lives within us. In so far as faith takes hold
of the living Christ alone, forgetful of its own quality
of strength or weakness, it grows God-pleasing activities, "the fruits of the Spirit," with the same naturalness
and spontaneity as an apple tree grows apples. When
self-centeredness has given way to Christ-centeredness,
our own standards, goals, motivations, all are obsolete.
What is humanly impossible becomes possible, for "I
can do all things through Christ who strengtheneth
me." "If any man be in Christ, he is a new creature."

Justification meant to Luther a rediscovery of this
Gospel in all its glorious power. His God was no intel-
lectual postulate or hypothesis but the mighty Lord of
Hosts who in Christ had dramatically invaded history

to wage a victorious battle against the forces of evil and who in faith is personally present to win the same victory in the life of an individual. It was this Christ who had overpowered a timid conscience-stricken monk and given him a radically new existence. The very terms "justice," "justification," and "faith" now took on a new vital connotation. "Justice," says Luther in his early *Lectures on Romans,* "is used in Scripture in a vastly different sense from its use by the philosophers and jurists."[13] He goes on to explain that in Scripture it means a redeeming and transforming righteousness. In a sermon a decade later he declares: "Note this fact carefully, that when you find in the Scriptures the word *God's justice* . . . it means the revealed grace and mercy of God through Jesus Christ."[14] Even the Melanchthonian key word "imputation" which was to mean so much in later orthodoxy appeared to him at times to be misleading because it expressed inadequately the work of Christ in justification: "There are some . . . who say 'the forgiveness of sins and justification depend entirely on divine imputation' . . . If this were true, the whole New Testament would be empty and vain. And Christ would have acted foolishly and uselessly in suffering for sinners. God himself would have engaged in needless deception and trickery, for even without Christ's suffering He could have forgiven sin or left it unreckoned, and then some other faith than faith in

---

[13] Ficker II, 121, 10.

[14] *Luther's Works* (Lenker ed.), X, sec. 37.

Christ could make us just and blessed, namely the kind of faith that commits itself to the mercy that does not reckon with sins."[15] Nor was faith to him any kind of static condition which could maintain its own continuity, an impersonal possession which could be hoarded. It is a person-to-person relation with Christ, which dissolves into nothingness unless it is vitalized by recurrent encounters with its living object. "Faith is a divine work in us. It changes us and makes us to be born anew of God. . . . It makes altogether different men, in heart and spirit and mind and powers, and it brings with it the Holy Ghost."[16] In the presence of God the believer sees in himself nothing but sin and in God nothing but forgiving and cleansing love. That this should be so is in itself grace, for to the extent in which we see ourselves free of sin we become self-sufficient and no longer need a Saviour. It is thus that faith lives in the constant tension of "simul iustus et peccator" and by the constant gift of forgiveness. Yet as the activity of God himself who fashions sinful men to be His working tools, faith is by its very nature dynamic and cannot but do good. It is the "foreman and captain" (*Werkmeister und Hauptmann*) of ethical activity.

The ethical implications of justification by faith have so often been obscured, even in Lutheran theology, that from the Roman theologians at the Council of Trent to Scheler, Troeltsch, and Tillich in our century,

---

[15] WA X, I, 468.
[16] WA X, I, 478.

critics have had occasion to construe it as only a formal juridical pronouncement impotent to generate moral power. Even Reinhold Niebuhr, who owes much to Luther in his diagnosis of man's sinful predicament, fails to do justice to the constructive power of grace and thus speaks of Lutheran quietism and defeatism which need at least to be supplemented from Renaissance sources. That faith releases tremendous energies for the renewal of life, both individual and social, or, in theological language, that justification is the basis for sanctification, is not so obvious when Luther's dynamic insights lie buried beneath the ponderous jargon of seventeenth-century forensics. And when, with the good intention of preventing the infiltration of synergistic errors, Lutheran theologians in their discussion of justification studiously avoid such words as "experience" and "ethical," it is easy to create the impression that the merits of Christ constitute a kind of paid-up insurance policy upon which the believer rests. When, finally, the influence of Lutheranism is judged, not in terms of what it has done in the countries of northern Europe where it has been the dominant force, but solely in its entangled German background, then misunderstanding reaches the point of making Luther responsible for Hitler. It is time for theologians everywhere to recognize that Karl Holl, not Ernst Troeltsch, is the correct interpreter of Luther's ethics and to rediscover with Holl the tremendous moral power in the Reformer's proclamation of sin and grace.   The vitalizing impact of the new Luther research in this field is felt in the English-speaking world principally through the ethical works of Emil Brunner, in which justification by faith is made the explicit starting point.

Unaffected by good report or evil, and whether the doctors agree or disagree, Luther himself would continue to validate his message by this simple criterion: "Even if St. Cyprian, St. Ambrose, or St. Augustine, even if St. Peter, St. Paul, or St. John, even if an angel from heaven, were to teach otherwise, nevertheless this I know for certain, that I do not teach that which is human but that which is divine, because I ascribe everything to God, nothing to men."[17] There is transforming power in the Gospel because the activity which it describes has God himself as the subject. Luther inspires us with the confidence that when sinful men, stripped of their pretensions, receive the Gospel, it is still the power of God "to efface sin, to destroy death, to remove curse, to bestow righteousness, to lift life to light, to deal out blessing."[18] In the simple words of the Catechism, "where there is forgiveness of sins, there is life." The man who has been taken off his own hands to live by God's grace walks, as Luther says, "the kingly road" between the Scylla of pride and the Charybdis of despair. Or as Paul would say it, "Having received this mercy, we faint not," we do not lose heart or nerve. The

[17] WA XL, I, 131.

[18] *Erlangen Ausgabe* of *Luther's Works*, Lat. Gal. 2, 21. Hereafter designated EA.

routine of everyday living with a high sense of respon-
life that flows from the forgiveness of sins invests the
sibility to God and to man, a steady poise, calm strength
and patience to bear burdens, one's own and those of
others, and an inner joy and gratitude which is independent of outward circumstances. In an hour of crisis
it produces the moral courage of a Munk, a Berggrav,
or a Niemoeller, or wells up in the power which undergirded the common people of Norway and of Finland
as they stood up to their oppressors with "A Mighty
Fortress is Our God" upon their lips.

The Gospel of regenerative grace has a direct relevance to the primary need of our day. This need is the
moral transformation of human nature. Without it all
our wisdom and all our power are worse than useless.
The greater the discoveries and the achievements of
the human spirit, the greater the curse they bring when
man does not use them right. The crisis occasioned by
the atom bomb rests fundamentally on the recognition
that no man and no group of men is good enough to be
entrusted with it. That Americans are no exception is
shown by the widespread opinion among us, voiced
even by some political leaders, that we ought to release
our atom bombs upon the Russians before they have
discovered the secret. When self-interest is endangered,
be it personal or national, there are no lengths to which
men will not go. Testifying at the trial of Petain, Leon
Blum declared, "I saw men change and become corrupted under my very eyes as if they had been plunged

into a bath of poison." Were there no "washing of regeneration and renewal of the Holy Ghost," the outlook would be dark indeed. The antidote proposed by
Max Otto, a typical American naturalistic philosopher,
"education in reverence for the human quest," is a poor
substitute, for the reverent attitude cannot long be
maintained unless the object of the quest is something
more and better than man himself. H. G. Wells, veteran
spokesman of the modern spirit, whose creative imagination many years ago envisaged the coming of the
atomic age, showed more penetrating realism in writing shortly before his death on "The Mind at the End
of its Tether." Surveying the panic, fanaticism, and
violence of mankind in the light of atomic fire, he saw
the coming of inevitable doom. And he knew no cogent
reason for persuading anyone that he should not be
mean, cruel, or cowardly. For himself, he "would rather
our species ended its story in dignity, kindliness, and
generosity, and not like drunken cowards in a daze, or
poisoned rats in a sack." The Christian young people
who met for an ecumenical youth conference in Amsterdam in the summer of 1939 had a preview of the same
horror picture when they compared mankind to the
crew of a sunken submarine who try to cheer one
another with candy and cigarettes. But the Christian
youth were also conscious of the only way out, rescue
from the outside. Against this background one can better appreciate Luther's message: "God wants to save
us not by our own but by extraneous justice and wis-

dom, by a justice that does not come from ourselves and does not originate in ourselves but comes to us from somewhere else."[19]

Eschatological in its basic outlook, the Gospel has from the outset taken full account of the thought of world-catastrophe, with "distress of nations, the sea and the waves roaring; men's hearts failing them for fear, and for looking after those things which are coming on the earth: for the powers of heaven shall be shaken" (Luke 21:25-26). But the Gospel never gives despair the last word, for it goes on to proclaim: "When these things begin to come to pass, then look up, and lift up your heads, for your redemption draweth nigh. . . . The Kingdom of God is nigh at hand." The doctrine of sin and grace is radical optimism against the background of radical pessimism. Those who accuse evangelical Christianity of defeatism have seen only one side of the picture. They fail to see that the same divine Word which annihilates also regenerates. They have not grasped that paradox of grace which, as Kierkegaard expresses it, finds "edification in the very thought that as against God we are always in the wrong." Far from implying, as is often supposed, a low and cringing estimate of man, this view invests man with the highest possible dignity, for it attaches full weight to human responsibility. He who shoulders this responsibility without wriggling from under its weight into the cheap rationalization "I am doing the best I can" discovers

---

[19.] Ficker I, 1.

that God gives such a dimension of depth to sin in order to show the still greater depth of His grace. Who has explored the strength for rich and wholesome living that is released by the forgiveness of sins? By what right do we go on supposing that the tuggings and strainings of our own moral will can generate more power than realignment to God? When have spontaneous joy and gratitude been weaker motives for righteousness than the forced and calculating efforts of self-will? Today when in the race against death men are once more putting their trust in the works-righteousness of more determined moral exhortation and more ambitious legislation, is there not reason to loose in all its undiluted strength the Gospel of justifying grace which gives power to become the sons of God?

4. We come to our fourth and final proposition in the meaning of justification: *The right relation to God results in the right relation to fellow-man.* Misled by Aristotelian eudaemonism, evangelical theologians ever since Melanchthon have tended to think of the end-result of justification in terms of eternal happiness for the individual and thus failed to place sufficient emphasis upon the inseparable connection in the Gospel between right relation to God and right relation to man. Just as love of God and love of neighbor form one indivisible command, so the prayer for the forgiveness by which our violation of God's will is pardoned contains a constant reference to our fellow-man: "as we forgive those who trespass against us." In a powerful

dramatization of this important truth in the parable of the merciless servant our Lord points out that divine forgiveness cannot be enjoyed unless it results in a forgiving disposition toward others. This emphasis did not escape Paul, the first theologian of justification: "As Christ forgave you, so must you forgive" (Col. 3:13, Moffatt translation). In rediscovering justification to be the heart of the Gospel Luther gave full weight to this aspect of its meaning. We are justified by faith, but faith, says the Reformer, "is nothing where love does not follow."[20] The two insights which Holl regards as Luther's greatest contributions to ethics, namely, a new conception of personality and a new conception of community, are bound together in the central doctrine of justification itself. Since we can give nothing to God but only receive from Him, we must do all our giving to our neighbor. God does not need what we have to give, but our neighbor does. The grace which breaks the grip of self-will empowers us for the service of love. Since Christ bears all our burdens, we are free to bear the burdens of others. The redeemed life is thus life in love, and God's true saints are to be found in a creative "communion of saints."

This new life in community is motivated from within by its own dynamic. In giving us His grace God also implants His own nature in us in the place of the old egocentric nature. Since God's nature, as Luther says, is "an abyss of pure love," "nothing but sheer doing of

---

[20] EA LII, 340.

good," neither is faith any state of rest but constant activity which engages in loving deeds as naturally as fire burns. Like God's own redeeming love, it is "round and whole," pouring itself out in glad spontaneity without any regard to the worth or worthlessness of its objects. Playing upon the double meaning of "equus," Luther calls the Christian "everybody's horse," one who gives equal service to enemy and to friend.[21]   In the Reformer's simple word "Love does whatever comes nearest,"[22] Brunner finds the living center of all evangelical ethics.[23]   It means that the neighbor is not a "case" to be dealt with according to a fixed law or program; he is a person toward whom you act in the way he needs and as you alone in your personal ministry of love can know. The faith that works through love is also the guiding principle in social organization. Luther rejects communism, because to be a Christian you must give, to give you must have, and to have you must find joy in doing your own God-given piece of work. When work is joyful worship of God and loving service of neighbor, it yields a sound self-respect which no parasite can enjoy. But the same consideration leads Luther to attack capitalistic greed. It is the duty of the Christian to give what he gains above his own reasonable needs to those less fortunate than himself. Just as God performs an "opus alienum," the foreign work of a

---

[21] WA III, 145.
[22] WA VI, 207.
[23] *The Divine Imperative,* tr. Olive Wyon (London: Macmillan, 1936), pp. 79, 591.

judge, to prepare the way for his "opus proprium" of a loving father, so a Christian uses worldly orders and callings and their "mammon of unrighteousness" for ultimate heavenly ends. Even the Christian's attitude toward himself must be governed by the law of love. That is the way Luther approaches the question of chastity and self-discipline. If I give way to sensuous indulgence, I cannot be of service to others. When faith is thus seen in the full range of its responsibilities, there is no aspect of either individual or communal life which it does not renew and energize.

It is in the field of human relations that the central principle of the Reformation shows its peculiar relevance to the needs of the present. "Every order of man's communal life," writes Dr. Charles Clayton Morrison, "stands today in need of regeneration by being confronted with the living God. Idols and idolatry everywhere infest our communal life.   The idolatry of the state, overthrown perhaps in those countries which yesterday were our enemies, threatens even our own democracy. The idolatry of power threatens our industrial order in the ego-centered conflict between capital and labor. The idolatry of money has long corrupted our culture. The idolatry of scientific knowledge has vitiated our education.   And now, as we are being ushered into the atomic age, we are in danger of being led into an idolatry of a world state endowed with power but lacking a religious faith to sustain it. The relevancy of Christianity has never been so manifest."[24]

These economic, political, and educational questions require more than economic, political, and educational answers. In a recent comment on the uplands of China, Dr. C. G. Shatzer, a geologist, made this statement: "Man has never found a way out when he has violated fundamental principles. When he has wantonly exploited natural resources he has had only depleted lands left, which cannot support the population. The inescapable result is a lower standard of living." The Christian Gospel declares that man has insoluble problems in all spheres because he has violated the most fundamental principle of his existence: life is God-dependent, not self-dependent. Hence the more determined the self-centered effort to save life, to fortify and elevate it, the more thorough the depletion. Even in case man does submit to something bigger than himself, if that something is less than divine, it turns out also to be nothing less than diabolical. The clearest demonstrations of this fact are afforded by the Nazi and Communist deifications of society with their enslavement of personality and distortion of true responsibility. The communal life, no less than individual life, needs to be judged and redeemed by the true God. Lesser solutions are, to use Karl Heim's metaphor, like replacing bulbs and twiddling with the switch when the fuse is blown and the lights are out. There will be no light until the connection with the source of light has been re-estab-

---

[24.] *The Christian Century,* March 13, 1946, p. 333.

lished. Justification by faith owes its perennial importance to the fact that it deals with this fundamental
connection. Even those who use this doctrine, as Reinhold Niebuhr does, only as an instrument of diagnosis,
to unearth the deepest source of our troubles, are ren-
dering important service. It is a needed corrective to
superficial moral idealism to show that the poison of
self-interest pervades the whole body politic so that
everything we do stands in need of forgiveness. The
mood of despair thus generated is doubtless nearer the
truth than the light-hearted optimism which accom-
panies a weak doctrine of sin. But despair, like unbelief, says Luther, is a great sin. It is a failure to grasp
the positive content of the Gospel. It represents that
impasse of purely rational thought expressed recently
by an American philosopher: "Loves beget jealousies
and divisions. Can unity be developed by anything but
authority or hate?" The answer lies in that higher love
which, unlike even the most refined human aspiration,
"envieth not" and "seeketh not its own" but forgives
and redeems, and therefore creates fellowship where
it did not exist before.

The axis of reality, taught William James, runs
through the hearts of individuals. This holds true also
in the relations between man and man. So long as a
man's actions are governed by a selfish pursuit of pleas-
ure or power, whatever his professed ideals may be,
such values as justice, love, and community remain
either abstract concepts or sentimental dreams. He

lacks the incentive to decision and commitment to translate them into personal reality. Such a translation takes place through that confrontation and cross-examination by God, for which justification stands. To stand conscience-bound in the presence of God, to give an account of oneself to Him, to think in terms of guilt and reconciliation, of sin and forgiveness, is to ascribe the greatest possible importance to personal relations. When through justification the center of gravity in these relations has shifted from self to God and to fellow-man, a true sense of responsibility is born. Man ceases to be indifferent to God and to neighbor and to use them as means of self-gratification. Sensitivity takes the place of indifference, and man becomes triumphantly dedicated to his proper function in the divine scheme of things: obedience to God and service to fellow-man. Freedom and democracy are now no longer empty slogans but take on a rich and vital content. Freedom is not the false liberty of irresponsible self-assertion but the glorious liberty of the children of God, the freedom to love and to serve. And equality and fraternity, the other ingredients of democracy, are similarly transfigured. Before God I stood not as an American or a German, a capitalist or a workingman, a doctor of philosophy or a grammar-school graduate, but as a man. Just so, in approaching my fellow-man, regardless of what labels may have been placed on him I shall not be misled into thinking of him as a mere type or representative of some impersonal or semi-

personal category. He is a man, as I am, for whom
Christ died as He did for me, and whose chief problem,
like mine, is to be reconciled to God. The soundest
spiritual groundwork for a realistic and thoroughgoing
democratic community of life, wherever man meets
man, is laid by the acknowledgment: Before the Law
of God "there is no difference, for all have sinned and
come short of the glory of God"; by the grace of God
there is no difference for "ye are all one in Christ Jesus."
To the latter end, those whom this Gospel reconciles to
God it also commissions to a ministry of reconciliation,
to be "little Christs" and mediators, applying the reconciling strategy of the Cross in every area of life to overcome sinful self-will and to untie the snarls it has left.
Universal spiritual priesthood is the social principle of
the Reformation, and it grows directly out of the material principle, justification by faith.

Conclusion. In an age in which the sin-defiled wisdom of man has perverted the power of nature unto
destruction, and nations are madly contesting for this
terrible secret, the Church has in the Gospel of justifying grace the secret of "the power of God unto salvation." It is as revolutionary in the sphere of religion and
morality as atomic energy is in military operations. "I
challenged an axiom," said Einstein in explaining his
discovery of relativity which opened the door into the
atomic age. Justification by faith challenges the basic
axiom of all natural goodness and holiness: good works
are necessary for salvation. It inverts this axiom to read:

salvation is necessary for good works. But the power of this inversion, or "foolishness" as he called it, enabled Paul to turn the ancient world upside down, to outlive, outdie, and outlast its principalities and powers. When the foolishness had been carefully removed and the Church had made its peace with the obvious, Luther rediscovered the great inversion, and once more the world shook with a spiritual explosion the tremors of which can still be felt. The method by which the power was released was quite analogous to the release of atomic energy. Caught in the cyclotron, an atom is tossed back and forth until it is charged with a hundred million volts and can penetrate another atom. Just so, an unsuspecting monk falls prey to God's trick, as he quaintly phrases it, is tossed back and forth in the cyclotron of conscience through long years of severe inner suffering until in every fibre of his being self-will is overcome and he knows nothing but Christ, and the Reformation is unloosed. In both cases the very structure of existence is tapped, in the former that of the physical universe, in the latter the ultimate source of all being, God himself whose nature it is to love and save sinners.

The historical significance of Luther's Gospel of justification by faith has often been better appreciated by its enemies than by its friends. Had not this barbarian appeared on the scene, averred Nietzsche, to ruin the Renaissance and to perpetuate Christianity, the devitalized medieval Church could not have prevented the total triumph of naturalistic Epicureanism. The same judgment is shared by Anatole France, who declared: "Jesus Christ owes it to this scamp of a friar that his shipwreck was put off for perhaps more than ten centuries."[25] These are blasphemous words but they bear out Luther's thesis: "the true treasure of the Church," the power by which it lives, is the Gospel.

Like Paul, Augustine, Luther, and Calvin, the outstanding protagonists of this Gospel, we too are living in a revolutionary age when a new world-epoch is in the making. But the strategy and battle array of the Christian Church are uncertain. Roman Catholicism is girding its loins for a mighty struggle with Communism for world mastery. Meanwhile the leaders of Protestantism, especially in America, are busy drawing up resolutions for a Christian reconstruction of society. No effort to combat anti-Christian forces, at home or abroad, by Catholics or by Protestants, is to be discounted. But the Church does not become clothed with power from on high by discarding the humble "form of a servant" worn by her Lord and putting on the more impressive vestments of cultural prestige and political influence. Needed external reforms will have to wait, as Luther said in speaking about economic affairs, "until our Lord God makes more Christians."[26] It is the mission of the Church to bear witness to that divine love which cannot wait until conditions have

---

[25] *La Révolte des Anges* (1914), p. 237.
[26] WA XII, 693.

been improved or even until the attitudes of men have changed, but takes the initiative, seeks the lost, encompasses the sinner in the midst of his sin, accepts the ungodly into fellowship with God. This witness rests upon the simple truth that man cannot find God until God has found him. There can be no penitence, no faith, and no holiness until a man has looked up into the face of the living Christ and found God there. The Church exists for the purpose of bringing together the conscience of man and the God who seeks him in Christ and thus bringing about the decision of commitment or repudiation. Yet even in the churches of the Reformation there appear to be few cases of clear-cut decision of either kind, compared with the prevalent confused and vague and therefore half-hearted religiosity of a general type or external participation in congregational and denominational activities. Why are men content with such second-bests when the Gospel we proclaim is the "good news" that Christ can be as livingly, intensely, and personally real to men of today as He was to the Apostles and the Reformers? Part of the answer is doubtless to be found in the godless spirit of the day which deadens conscience and causes many professing Christians to be actually pagans at heart. But a large share of the responsibility must rest also with our ministry itself. Have we not made of the heart of the Gospel, justification by faith, a museum piece which is dusted off and exhibited on Reformation Day and then placed back on the shelf? During the rest of the year do we not too often allow people to keep the impression that if they live the best they know how God will not be too strict with them but in His kindness will make up what they lack? Have we not been satisfied with a church membership made up of nice, respectable people rather than regenerated people? Have we not virtually abandoned to sectarian zealots such essential aspects of Christianity as doctrine of the Holy Spirit and His power to change the hearts of men?

Effective preaching of justification requires both a firm grasp of fundamental theology and the keenest possible insight into human nature. Vital importance attaches to such doctrinal distinctions as those between the Law and the Gospel and between justification and sanctification. Failure to distinguish properly between the Law and the Gospel has led many a would-be minister of the Gospel or evangelist to present faith as a demand and a condition of salvation and even to use coercive methods to produce it. The result is legalistic exertion born of fear, not the joyful spontaneity of faith. And when admonitions to holy living are addressed to people with no knowledge or experience of justification, the result is a moralistic perversion of the Gospel. The true minister of the Gospel, then, must know not only the Gospel itself in its purity but also his people in the variety of their individual experience and attitudes. Rightly to divide the word of truth so as to bring God and man face to face requires individual soul-care and life-situation preaching and teaching. It is much easier to offer solutions to the problems of society and of the universe than it is to help a man or woman to solve the problem of a personal adjustment to God. But the spiritual revolution which the world needs to make the solution of its problems more than mere theory will not come until more Sauls, overpowered by God, are changed into Pauls who can victoriously say: "Therefore being justified by faith, we have peace with God through our Lord Jesus Christ, by whom also we have access by faith into this grace wherein we stand, and rejoice in hope of the glory of God" (Rom. 5:1-2).

CHAPTER III

THE LIVING WORD AND THE PRESENT NEED

JUSTIFICATION by faith is the basic principle of the Gospel and therefore also of all evangelical theology. It is nothing less than the heart of the Gospel itself, the theological epitomization of the good news which makes the Gospel what it is and the proclamation of which gives the Church its right to exist. Theology, as Paul Althaus has said, is simply "the completion of the act of faith in the sphere of thought."[1] Vital theology, then, like vital preaching, is never a mere juxtaposition of propositions, no matter how important or true. All the truths it presents radiate from one living center. It is thus that we must conceive the relationship between justification, the material principle of the theology of the Christian Gospel, and its other two cardinal principles, the authority of the Word, the formal principle, and universal spiritual priesthood, the ethical and social principle. As regards the formal principle, to which we now turn our attention, it is important to recognize from the outset that both historically and logically, for the Reformers as well as for the Apostles, the dynamic

---

[1] *Evangelium und Leben* (1927), p. 26.

center of the Gospel, the sin-forgiving and faith-awakening grace of God, comes first, and the Word obtains its significance as the means by which this grace is mediated. If the Word were essentially a body of doctrines or ideas and faith the intellectual assent to these ideas, then the reverse procedure would hold. It would be necessary first to demonstrate the authoritativeness of the source of the ideas in order to secure conviction. But when with Luther we listen in the Word to "the Gospel of God concerning His Son," and with Paul experience the Gospel to be "the power of God unto salvation," then the worth and the authoritativeness of the Word require no extraneous support, for the Word validates itself as the vehicle of grace.

Such a concept of the Word is free from all artificial and impersonal "bookishness." Its authority rests not on what men think or say about it but upon what it does to men. Unlike its rival, the Roman papacy, the Word does not need to be undergirded by a man-made dogma about its infallibility, for it ushers men into God's own presence. Unlike the Koran, the Granth, and the Book of Mormon, the Scripture bearing that Word does not need to bolster its credibility with extravagant claims of having come down miraculously from heaven. It proves its divine origin by furnishing actual contacts with God. In brief, this dynamic concept of the Word of God describes nothing less than the Holy Spirit in action, addressing each man as an individual "thou" and calling him to confront the judging and redeeming God in terms of personal responsibility. Let us, then, study this fundamental evangelical principle of the living Word, (1) as it appears in the New Testament and in early Christianity, (2) as it was rediscovered by Luther, and (3) as it needs to be rediscovered in our day.

I. THE WORD IN PRIMITIVE CHRISTIANITY

When our Lord had finished the Sermon on the Mount, so Matthew tells us, His hearers, deeply stirred, said to one another: "He teaches as one who has authority. He does not speak as our scribes." Like the professional exegetes, the scribes, Jesus too had quoted Old Testament Scripture and had even subscribed to the prevalent rabbinical teaching that not one jot or tittle of the Law could be destroyed. But the people who heard Jesus sensed a vast difference between the customary exposition of the sacred writings, no matter on how high a pedestal it placed them, and the vital Word spoken by Jesus. They were aware that on the lips of Jesus the Word of God had somehow become alive, so that in the words spoken by this man God himself had spoken. The same reaction was elicited on other occasions. "No man ever spoke like this man!" "God has visited his people!"

In seeking to explain this consciousness of the immediate presence of God so strongly felt by the Speaker and so effectively communicated to His hearers, it was natural that the latter were led to think of the prophets, those inspired men of God in the past, upon whom God himself had laid His hand, usually against their own natural inclinations, and upon whose lips He had placed His own message, so that they no longer used the worn stereotypisms of standardized religion but spoke God's direct answer to the needs of the day. Thus centuries after the voice of the last of the acknowledged prophets had become silent, Jesus' contemporaries said of Him, "A great prophet has arisen in our midst." Those who knew their prophets best were reminded specifically of Jeremiah, the greatest of all the prophets. His message of the inwardness of true religion, the new covenant made with the individual, not with the nation, and the new law written on the heart, not on tablets of stone, coupled with an overpowering sense of divine commission which had to be carried out in spite of the personal tragedy involved, all this appeared to be re-enacted in the message and mission of the Man of Nazareth. When, however, that mission had been fulfilled through its final phases of the crucifixion, the resurrection, the ascension, and the coming of the Spirit, those who had come to know Him, not merely according to the flesh, but according to the Spirit, and had come to share the power of His resurrection, knew: Here is more than a prophet. Here is Immanuel, God incarnate. God indeed had spoken "at sundry times and in divers manners" to the fathers through the prophets, but in His Son He actually came.

The apostolic message thus obtains its content. Christ is not only a revealer of God. He is the revelation. He not only speaks God's Word. He is the Word. Paul repeatedly drives this truth home with sharp staccato statements: "We preach Christ." "God was in Christ." "In him are hid all the treasures of wisdom and knowledge." "In him dwells the fullness of the godhead bodily." "In him all things were created." " . . . the King of ages, immortal, invisible, the only God." In the Johannine writings an explicit identification of Christ with the Word of God takes place. "In the beginning was the Word . . . the Word was God . . . the Word became flesh and dwelt among us." "That which was from the beginning, which we have heard, which we have seen with our eyes, which we have looked upon and touched with our hands, concerning the word of life" (I John 1:1). "He is clad in a robe dipped in blood and the name by which he is called is the Word of God" (Rev. 19:13). The person of Him who had said, "I am the truth," is inseparable from His message. He is the light that enlightens every man, making the meaning of nature intelligible, disclosing the ground-plan of the universe. History, too, remains a closed book until the Lamb who is the Logos opens its seals.

The uniqueness of this apostolic identification of the Word of God with the Son of God lies in its thoroughly personal and dynamic character. Israel had long known: "By the word of the Lord were the heavens made." "He spoke and it was done." The Targums, the Aramaic versions of the Old Testament, use the principle of "memra" or executive word of God as the mediator between God and the world, and it is to the "memra," not to God himself, that all God's contacts with men are ascribed. The prophets had indeed proclaimed a God who actively directs the course of history, and the apocalyptists, the successors of the prophets, had sought to keep alive the hope in the coming of the Messiah, God's personal representative in history. But by the time of Jesus the religion of Israel had become a religion of the Book, and the accepted medium of divine revelation was the written document rather than the inspired personality. Unable to make any meaningful contact with God in contemporary history, men had become satisfied with affirming: God has spoken to the fathers in the past, and His will has become permanently codified for us in Holy Writ. It was during the post-Exilic period and under the influence of the Greek idea of divination that the sacred writers of the past came to be considered as the amanuenses of God, transcribers of divine dictation.

Against this background we can appreciate the freshness and the vitality of the apostolic concept of the Word. In a day in which the traditional religion was expressed in such statements as, "This is the Book of the commandments of God and the law that endureth forever; all they that hold it fast are appointed to life, but such as leave it shall die" (Baruch 4:1), the apostles had a living Gospel, a sure word of hope for the condemned. It issued not from a book but from the incarnate Word "in whom was life." They themselves had

had first-hand contact with this Word of Life and were witnesses to the way in which He had made God real to them. The truth which they proclaimed was not an impersonal something to be understood and pondered about. It was a gift to be received, a life to be lived, a Master to be joyfully followed even to death. It centered around a living Person in whom God had become alive and established personal fellowship with them. Its credential was the messianic power which accompanied its proclamation. This type of verification had been used by the Lord himself in answering John the Baptist's inquiry as to the authenticity of His messiahship: "Go and tell John the things which ye hear and see: the blind receive their sight, and the lame walk, the lepers are cleansed, and the deaf hear, and the dead are raised up, and the poor have the gospel preached to them" (Matt. 11:4-5). The apostles too, Peter and John as well as Paul, look upon Christ as God's own creative power in redemptive action, and discover in the Gospel the divine energy by which men are born anew. "By his great mercy we have been born anew" (I Peter 1:3). "To all who received him . . . he gave power to become children of God, who were born . . . of God" (John 1:12). The "word of truth" and the "'power of God" accompany each other (II Cor. 6:7). "My speech and my message," says Paul, "were not in plausible words of wisdom, but in demonstration of the Spirit and power" (I Cor. 2:2). Natural unregenerate reason not only fails to find God; it also fails to see in the Gospel anything but foolish nonsense. But from the view-point of that person-to-person encounter with God called faith, the Gospel is both ultimate truth, "the wisdom of God," and supreme value, "the power of God." Just as the center of the Pauline message is the living Christ, so "the power of God" flows specifically from Christ's resurrection and manifests itself in a duplication of the Easter miracle in the risen life of the believer.

The dynamic Christ-centered nature of the apostolic message precluded any overemphasis upon the written form of the Word. The burden of the apostolic witness was not "God wrote a book" but "God sent forth his Son." Primitive Christianity, unlike post-Exilic Judaism, was certainly not primarily a book-religion. Jesus himself wrote nothing, neither did most of the apostles. The great commission, "As the Father has sent me, even so I send you" meant "Proclaim the Gospel to every creature," "Make all men my disciples," but it gave no special priority to the literary craftsmen or to the bookbinders. The disciples went forth, not with rolls of papyri under their arms but with the Spirit in their hearts and the living Gospel on their lips. The same Spirit later moved some of them and some of their associates and converts to bear the same witness through writing. The written Word and the spoken Word came from the same source, the Spirit of the risen Christ at work in the Christian fellowship. The writings of the New Testament constitute for us, as for all ages, the

most direct access to original Christianity and as such
have the highest possible importance. But it would be
presumptuous to hold, for example, that the Word
spoken by Paul at Miletus to the Elders of Ephesus,
reported only in brief by Luke and containing such
characteristic expressions as "testifying both to Jews
and to Greeks" of "repentance to God and of faith in
our Lord Jesus Christ," "I do not account my life of any
value . . . if only I may accomplish my course," and
"feed the Church of the Lord which he obtained for
himself with his blood," represented a lower order of
inspiration than the *written* epistles in which he uses
the same expressions. Nor is there any reason to suppose that the inspiration which we ascribe to Paul's
preaching as recorded by Luke differed from that
which motivated his unrecorded preaching. For many
centuries, indeed, until the New Testament canon was
formed, the Church lived by the Word and proclaimed
it, although it had no sacred writings of its own. It
simply adopted the Bible of the Jews and called it its
Old Testament. To obtain a Christian concept of the
Word of God it is highly instructive to observe why
this was done. The Christians did not believe in Christ
chiefly because of the Old Testament; they believed in
the Old Testament because of Christ. The Lord himself
was not only deeply rooted in the Old Testament, but
He saw it pointing to Himself and considered His
whole mission to be a fulfillment of its law, prophecy,
and sacrificial system. Thus while the Jews to this day

believe the Old Testament but do not thereby arrive at faith in Christ, the apostolic Christians reversed the entire procedure and valued the Old Testament because they found Christ there. Actually the Hebrew Scriptures thus became a new book, a book explicable only in terms of Christ. And whether it is definitely acknowledged or not, a critical principle of evaluation has thus been introduced whereby those portions of the Old Testament which have little reference to Christ have correspondingly little value.

One further aspect in the dynamic character of the apostolic concept of the Word must be noted. It is the temporal antecedence and permanent high function of the *visible* Word, the sacraments. Long before the Church had any New Testament writings or had decided upon any canon of Scripture, Christians entered into a vital personal relationship with their Lord through the baptismal washing of regeneration, and strengthened and deepened that relationship through receiving the bread and wine of the Eucharist. Here the Christ-centered dynamism of the Gospel finds perfect expression. The sacraments point back directly to Christ himself, who is their author and through them communicates His own living presence. Here is genuine "existential communication." Christ, the incarnate Word, addresses Himself in a process at once physical and spiritual to the whole personality of the individual, body as well as soul. In the person-to-person encounter of faith the believer takes hold of the Lord himself, not just something said or written about Him. As Paul expresses it, in baptism he "puts on Christ," in the Eucharist he "participates in Christ." "The highest," said Goethe, "cannot be spoken." The inference is that it must be dramatized rather than verbalized. Pointing to the dynamic drama of the sacraments we may appropriately use the prophetic saying: "*See* ye the Word of the Lord" (Jer. 2:31).

Not only in the explicit teaching of the apostles themselves but also in the "testimonium primitivae ecclesiae," so highly prized by the Reformers, the dynamic view of the Word is clearly in the ascendant. As carriers of the Word, the early Christians were primarily witnesses, living "epistles of Christ," rather than dealers in documents. The secret of their influence lay in the fact that their allegiance was to a Person and a Presence, not to a protocol or system. Motivated and guided by the Spirit, clothed with "power from on high," they were prepared to seal their testimony with their blood, to be "slain for the Word of God" (Rev. 6:9). As in the onward march of history the days when the incarnate Word himself walked on the earth receded into the past, the objective content of the Christian message came to depend more and more upon the written record left by such men as Luke, who had "undertaken to compile a narrative of the things accomplished" among them. But the church of the martyrs was not inclined to change the apostolic emphasis "Faith comes from hearing" into "Faith comes from reading." The *Didache*, a second-century document, declares emphatically: "Thou shalt night and day remember him who *speaks* to thee the word of God; thou shalt honor him as the Lord, for whence the word of the Lord is *spoken*, there the Lord is." And Eusebius, the first church historian, quotes the second-century Father, Papias, as saying, "I do not derive as much benefit from books as from the voice of living persons."[2] The reference to books is to Scriptures. Whether or not this was the prevailing view, it is certain at all events that the content of the Word, Christ and His life-changing Gospel, was in the foreground, not any vehicle of its transmission. According to apostolic witness itself, the written Word, like every activity of the Spirit, demonstrates its divine origin and authenticity by what it does: it teaches, reproves, corrects, trains in righteousness, that the man of God may be complete, equipped for every good work (II Tim. 3:17). It is a far cry from the age of the apostles and of the martyrs when men wrest the words "All Scripture is God-inspired" from this dynamic context, focus attention upon the means rather than the end, and construct theories about the uniqueness of the writing process.

During the first four centuries of its existence the Church had a rich heritage of sacred writings but no standardized Scripture. Justin Martyr's Bible consisted of the Old Testament and the four gospels. The New Testament of Tertullian and of Irenaeus contained 22 books, that of Origen 29, that of Clement of Alexandria

---

[2] Eusebius, *Hist. Eccl.* III, 39, 4.

30. Many of the Fathers accepted the Shepherd of Hermas as Scripture, and many rejected the Epistle to the Hebrews. The final form gradually assumed by the New Testament canon was determined not so much by the work of the official councils as by the same principle which Paul set up as the criterion of the spoken Word, the power to edify (I Cor. 14). While no absolute uniformity exists in the gospels themselves even about such basic matters as the form of the Lord's prayer or the words of the institution of the Eucharist, no need was felt for a "harmony of the gospels." The important thing was the witness itself, the proclamation of "the eternal life which was with the Father and was made manifest" (I John 1:2), and the spiritual power it brought. Thus, for example, according to St. Cyprian, the reward of him who studies Scripture is that "greater power shall be granted to him."[3] And St. Gregory of Nazianzus, condemning those who "are overmuch concerned with the letter which holds you as its slave," concentrates on the work of the Spirit, who "if He find fishermen at their work, sweeps them into the net of Christ to bring the whole world within the meshes of the Word" and "if He finds men enthusiastic for persecution . . . transforms their energy, and out of a Saul He fashions a Paul."[4] The dynamic concept of the Word held by the Fathers finds perhaps its finest ex-

---

[3.] *Test.*, Book I, Introd.

[4.] Quoted in G. D. Barry, *The Inspiration and Authority of Holy Scripture* (London: S.P.C.K., 1919), p. 107.

pression in St. Irenaeus, who clearly anticipates the specific view of Luther in using the New Testament as the guide to the Old, in presenting faith as the subjective correlate of Scripture, and in holding that Scripture, viewed with Christ in its center, is self-interpreting. We may appropriately close this section of our study with two statements from Irenaeus: the Scriptures "are perfect, because they were spoken by the Word of God and His Spirit"[5] and "Where the Church is, there is the Spirit of God, and where the Spirit of God, there the Church and every grace; but the Spirit is truth."[6]

II. LUTHER'S REDISCOVERY OF THE LIVING WORD

It is common knowledge that the Lutheran Reformation elevated the Word of God to the position of supreme authority and that Lutheranism in its essential content is a "theology of the Word." What is not so generally known or appreciated is the fact that Luther did not make a simple identification of the Word of God with the text of the Bible and therefore did not set up a "paper pope" in the place of the Roman pontiff. Luther's life work owes its permanent vitality to his rediscovery, in all its power, of the living Word of the apostolic age, which confronts man, calls for personal decision, and when that decision is the commitment of faith, transforms and energizes man. Luther's unchain-

---

[5] *Adv. Her.*, II, 28, 2.
[6] *Ibid.*, III, 24, 1.

ing of the Bible has often been misinterpreted. In its accepted Latin version, the Vulgate, the Bible was in wide use throughout the Church, and various translations into the vernacular, including the German, were already extant. Theologians had already appealed to the Bible as to the supreme arbiter in doctrinal disputes. This was especially true of the Nominalistic school of Occam in its controversies with the traditional Aristotelian Scholasticism. And the Church as a whole recognized the Bible as a doctrinal and moral authority of equal weight with the unwritten tradition and the established government of the Church. The peculiarity of the Reformers' view lies in the sovereign all-sufficiency of Scripture, expressed by the term "sola scriptura," which in turn rests upon its vital connection with "solus Christus," "sola gratia," and "sola fide." It is because Scripture brings us face to face with Christ, is the means of grace, and the generator of saving faith, that it is the one adequate authority. The Occamists, like the later Protestant scholastics, used the Bible as an arsenal of authoritative proof-texts. And the whole Roman church, in the words of Karl Barth, had "sequestered the Word of God beforehand for herself by an embargo and taken it under her own management, and lost the capacity of listening to the voice of a Confronter."[7] By denying the Bible any authority above that of the popes and the councils and by lording it

---

[7] *Doctrine of the Word of God* (New York: Scribner's, 1936), p. 306.

over the Word itself, the Roman church has in fact no transcendental source of power or authority above its own historical existence.

In the course of the Reformation Luther was compelled, fighting his own natural disposition all the way, to reject the final authority of both the papacy and the councils. But he did not arrive at the doctrine of the sole authority of Scripture by the simple negative method of elimination. Some years before the beginning of the Reformation, probably in 1513 or 1514, he had had a profound religious experience, the so-called "tower-experience," by which in his own life doubt had given way to certainty and joyful personal fellowship with God had been established. Of permanent significance is the fact that this experience came not through mystical or ascetic exercises, ecclesiastical rites, moral effort, or philosophical speculation, but through an insight into the meaning of Scripture. It was in Scripture, in Psalm 31:1, "Deliver me in thy righteousness," that he found the articulate expression for the deepest cause of his soul-torment: How can I, a sinner, ask a righteous God for deliverance? But it was Scripture also, Rom. 1:17, which gave the answer, resolved the tension and gave him the peace of God: "For in it the righteousness of God is revealed through faith for faith; as it is written, 'He who through faith is righteous shall live.'" The message of the Reformation, justification through faith, was thus drawn from Scripture, but not as a cool academic deduction. It came as God's own

answer to distressed conscience. It meant, in Luther's
words, that "the face of the Scriptures was changed."
The Bible was no longer a mere book, a repository of
information and advice. It was the source of spiritual
insight and power, the means by which God gives us
Christ. The rediscovery of the faith by which the
apostles lived was thus also a rediscovery of the living
Word by which that faith is generated. The intimate
connection between the material and the formal principles of the Reformation, which makes it impossible
to understand the one without the other, becomes clear
when we examine Luther's concept "sola scriptura" in
its relationship to each of the three pronouncements by
which Lutheran theology expresses the content of justification, "solus Christus," "sola gratia," and "sola fide."

Consider first "solus Christus." Lutheranism is radically Christ-centered, for, like the apostles, it knows
"no other name by which we must be saved." But precisely here, according to Luther, is the one and only
function of the Bible and the ground of its authority:
it gives us Christ. The Reformer could hardly have
been more explicit or emphatic than he was on this
central issue. "I do not understand anything in Scripture except Christ the Crucified." "Christ is the sum
and truth of the Scriptures." "The entire Scripture
points only to Christ." "Take Christ out of the Bible,
and what is left?"[8] In picturesque language Luther portrays the Bible as "the swaddling cloth and the manger

---

[8] WA IV, 153; WA III, 620; WA XII, 73; EA VII, 125.

in which Christ lies." He is fully aware of the human side of the Bible. "Crude and mean (*schlecht und geringe*) is the swaddling cloth," "but precious is the treasure, Christ, which therein lies."[9] Luther rises to the genuine apostolic heights of identifying this precious treasure, Christ, with the essential meaning of the Word. "You must yourself in your conscience feel Christ himself and unshakably experience that it is God's word, even if the whole world fought against it."[10] We need but call to mind the familiar words of *Ein' feste Burg:*

> "The *Word* they still shall let remain,
> Nor any thanks have for it.
> *He* (not *it*) is by our side upon the plain
> With His good gifts and Spirit."

Luther's thoroughly dynamic Christ-centered approach to the Bible left him remarkably free as regards the text of the Scriptures. The more his conscience was bound to that Word of God which is Christ, the less it was bound to externals. Hence he had no compunctions about calling the swaddling cloth "crude and mean." His mission was to glorify the Christ, not the swaddling cloth. The problem of the fundamentalists of our day, the defense of the errorlessness of the written documents, simply did not exist for him. Thus, for example, in commenting on the fact that Matthew attributes the text of the thirty pieces of silver to Jeremiah although

---

[9] EA XLIII, 8.
[10] EA XXVIII, 289.

the quotation is from Zechariah, Luther says, "This and similar questions do not mean much to me, since they are of no particular profit, and Matthew has done enough when he has cited a genuine text even if he does not have the correct name. . . . We can pass that by. . . . And that is the manner of all apostles who do the same thing, citing statements of Scripture without such meticulous care concerning the text."[11] In another connection he declares, "When discrepancies occur in Holy Scriptures and we cannot harmonize them, let it pass, it does not endanger the article of the Christian faith, because all the evangelists agree in this, that Christ died for our sins."[12] With such an attitude he is free to say in a sermon, "John is confused here,"[13] and to criticize Paul's use of the allegorical method in the fourth chapter of Galatians. The Christocentric principle not only guides him in his interpretation of the Bible but also leads him to challenge the right of entire books within it to be considered Scripture at all. The Book of Esther, for example, has such a far-fetched connection with Christ that Luther wished that it had "not come to us at all." As to the Epistle of James, not only did he refer to it in 1522 as "a straw epistle" but as late as 1540, six years before his death, he exploded with: "Some day I will use James to fire my stove."[14]

[11] WA XXIII, 642.
[12] WA XLVI, 726.
[13] WA XXVIII, 269.
[14] WA *Tischreden*, 5854.

The attempt of the late Dr. Reu to reconcile such statements with a fundamentalist position, on the ground that Luther regarded James as noncanonical, begs the entire question, for it was the alleged lack of Christ-centered content which led Luther to deny the canonicity of James and of other books. It is strange reasoning indeed to insist on the absolute inerrancy of the Bible in the smallest details and from cover to cover, and yet to follow and defend a leader who rejected whole books within it as unfit to be considered the Word of God. Does the principle, "The Scripture cannot be broken," apply to words and letters but not to entire writings? The only way out is simply to admit: Luther will not fit into a fundamentalist straitjacket. Not many of us today agree completely with Luther's views on canonics, but we should all appreciate the seriousness of his appeal from the letter of the Bible to the living Lord of the Bible.

The second word in the message of the Reformation is "sola gratia." It is the good news "By grace you are saved"; the Christ whom we proclaim is not a lawgiver but a forgiver. But this Gospel is precisely what the Word of God meant to Luther. "The Word of God," he defines explicitly, "is the Gospel of God concerning His Son."[15] He makes the same assertion conversely, "The Gospel is not only what Matthew, Mark, Luke, and John have written. . . . The Gospel is the Word about the Son of God who became flesh, suffered, was glori-

---

[15.] "Christian Liberty," *Works* (Holman ed.), II, 315.

fied. . . . The Gospel is the Word of God."[16] This distinctively Lutheran conception of the Word is confessionally stated in the *Apology*, where the Gospel of justifying grace is called the key which "alone opens the door to the whole Bible" and in the *Formula of Concord*, which declares: "Therefore we reject and regard incorrect and injurious the dogma that the Gospel is properly a preaching of repentance or reproof, and not alone a preaching of grace. For thereby the Gospel is again converted into a law, the merit of Christ and the Holy Scriptures obscured, Christians robbed of true consolation, and the door opened again to the papacy." In our century it has received clear expression in the Baltimore Declaration of the United Lutheran Church: "We believe that, in its most real sense, the Word of God is the Gospel, i.e., the message concerning Jesus Christ, His life, His work, His teachings, His suffering and death, His resurrection and ascension for our sakes, and the saving love of God thus made manifest in Him."

When the Word is defined in terms of the person and work of Christ and of the saving love of God, it necessarily assumes a dynamic character. Commandments and precepts are static, but grace is ongoing and transforming activity. So powerful is this living Word in original Lutheranism that not even the subsequent orthodoxists, who identified the Word with the sacred writings and gave rise to the hypothesis that the purest

---

[16.] Ficker, II, 12 ff.

Word of God is to be found in the lost and buried documents of the original biblical manuscripts, could successfully embalm it. Even when in actual practice faith meant little more than intellectual assent to pure doctrine, that doctrine retained at least theoretically the dogma that the Word is the "means of grace" and that one of the properties of the Bible is its "efficacy." In Luther's ministry the Word as means of grace was no empty figure of speech. It represented not "Deus dixit," a God who had once spoken, caused His voice to be recorded, and then become silent, but "Deus loquens," the God who continues to speak. His Word is not confined to what the prophets and the apostles had written. Luther summarizes thus his own life work: "I simply taught, preached, wrote God's Word."[17] And such is the high mission of every minister of the Gospel: "Who speaks Christ's Word may freely boast that his mouth is Christ's mouth."[18] I know of no loftier or more vital conception of the Gospel ministry than the one contained in the following words of Luther: "A preacher should declare reassuringly with St. Paul and all the apostles and prophets: 'Haec dixit Dominus, God himself has said this.' And again: 'In this sermon I have been an apostle and prophet of Jesus Christ.' Here it is not necessary, nor even good, to ask for the forgiveness of sins. For it is God's Word, not mine, and so there can be no reason for His forgiving me; He can

---

[17.] *Works* (Holman ed.), II, 399.
[18.] WA VIII, 683.

only confirm and praise what I have preached, saying:
'Thou hast taught correctly, for I have spoken through
thee, and the Word is mine.' Anyone who cannot say
this of his own preaching should stop, for he must
surely be lying and blaspheming God when he
preaches."[19]

Special attention must be given to Luther's emphasis
upon oral proclamation as the distinctive medium of
the Word of the Gospel. Because this emphasis is so
important in Luther's conception of the "living" Word
and because it has been largely forgotten in the later
identification of divine revelation with the written
Word, let me quote Luther at some length on this matter. "For in the New Testament preaching," says the
Reformer, "preaching should be made orally public
with a living voice and bring forth to speech and hearing what hitherto is hidden in the letters and secret
aspect. Since the New Testament is nothing else than
an opening and revealing of the Old Testament. . . .
Therefore even Christ himself did not write down His
teaching, as Moses did his, but did it orally and likewise commanded it to be done orally and gave no command to write it. Moreover, the apostles also wrote
little, and not all of them did that. . . . Therefore it is
not like the New Testament to write books about Christian doctrine, but there should be, without books, in all
places good, instructed, spiritual, diligent preachers
who draw the living word out of the ancient writ and

[19.] WA LI, "Wider Hans Worst."

unceasingly din it into people, as the apostles did. For before they wrote they first had preached to and converted the folk by the living voice, which was also their proper apostolic and New Testament work. . . . But man's need to write books is a great injury, and it is a violation of the Spirit that the need has compelled it and is not the way of the New Testament."[20] Luther goes on to present the thought that the principal function of the written Word is the negative one of defense against corruption, while the positive task of presenting Christ and awakening faith belongs primarily to the oral Word. While his defense of the pure Gospel against the false mysticism of the "Schwaermer" thus led him to an increasingly higher valuation of the written Word, his original inclination was to correlate the written Word with the Old Testament and the spoken Word with the New. To the passage above, taken from an Epiphany sermon, may be added the following excerpt from his commentary on Peter: "Thus the books of Moses and the prophets are also the Gospel, since they have proclaimed and described beforehand concerning Christ, precisely what the apostles have preached or written afterwards. Yet there is a distinction between them. For as both according to the letter are written on paper, nevertheless the Gospel or New Testament should really not be written, but be put into the living voice, which then resounds and is heard everywhere in the world. But that it is also written has

[20] WA X, 625 ff.

happened superfluously. But the Old Testament is composed only in writing, and therefore it is called 'a letter' and so the apostles call it 'the writ,' for it has only pointed to the coming Christ. But the Gospel is a living sermon by Christ."[21] So dynamic is the Gospel of grace that no letter, not even the letter of Holy Writ, appears to be adequate to convey it. The living Word requires its own dynamic medium, the living voice.

Having discussed "solus Christus" and "sola gratia," we need not dwell at length on the obvious connection between "sola scriptura" and "sola fide." Faith is simply Christ and His grace viewed from the subjective or experiential side. The Word demonstrates its aliveness by being the generator of living faith. Christ gives us not only His Word but also through the Word His Spirit by which the true significance of the Word is known, if it is to be known at all. Thus in his exposition of the Psalms, Luther interprets "Give me understanding" (Ps. 119:34) as meaning, Give me the Holy Spirit; for the letter of the Scripture as such does not contain understanding. And "Make me live" (Ps. 119:17) means, Give me faith; for it is through faith that the living Christ comes to dwell in the believer. In another connection Luther puts it this way: "One who does not know Christ may hear the Gospel or hold the book right in his hands, but he does not yet have understanding of it, for to have the Gospel without understanding is to have no Gospel. And to have the Scripture without

²¹· WA XII, 275.

knowledge of Christ is to have no Scripture."[22]   Karl
Barth expresses this thought well: "The statement, 'The
Bible is God's Word,' is a confession of faith, a statement made by the faith that hears God himself speak
in the human word of the Bible."[23] The *indirectness* of
revelation, stressed by Barth and Kierkegaard, the fact
that God conceals Himself, even in His Word, behind
an unpretentious exterior which only faith can penetrate, has a strong foundation in Luther. This is the significance, for our present discussion, of the "theologia
crucis" which Luther preferred to a "theologia gloriae."
We cannot speak about God as He is in the majesty of
His glory but only as faith sees Him "in the Virgin's
lap, on the Cross, . . . in the Word."[24]   False theology,
guided by reason, can apply to God only terms which
everybody recognizes as high and glorious. True theology, guided by faith, takes hold of God even though
He is hidden beneath the rags of weakness, disgrace,
and suffering. In this perspective we can see how little
the Word, understood as Luther understood it, has to
fear from any biblical criticism. It is more consistent
with the "theology of the Cross" to expect God to speak
through a medium in which reason sees human limitations than through one which can be rationally demonstrated to be inerrant. The theory of biblical infallibility
may thus turn out to be but another attempt to remove

[22.] WA X, 628.

[23.] *Op. cit.*, p. 123.

[24.] WA XXVIII, 135

the offense of the Cross. The connection between "sola scriptura" and "sola fide" may be seen finally also in Luther's use of the so-called "tropological" principle in the interpretation of Scripture. It means that Christ himself is actually present in faith and that the faith-awakening Word becomes more than a record of what He has done, even more than the voice of God telling what Christ has done. It becomes Christ's own redeeming activity taking place in the heart of the believer here and now.

III. THE PRESENT NEED
FOR REDISCOVERING THE LIVING WORD

We come to grips now with the question: Is there need for rediscovering and re-emphasizing the living dynamic Word of the apostles and of Luther in our day? In seeking to present an affirmative answer to this question we are not forgetting that authentic theology hearkens to God, not to men, and hence draws its content from enduring divine truth, not from the changing needs of various ages. But our survey of the past teaches precisely this lesson: the divine truth does not endure as a static quantum, possessed and hoarded and handed down from one generation to another, but as a series of personal encounters by which men of each successive generation face God himself, hear His voice and receive His life-changing power. The lasting significance of the Bible is that it is not only a record of such encounters in the past but also the means by which the Spirit who inspired the original witnesses makes His vital impact upon men of every age. Thus we may say with Professor H. M. Mueller that the proclamation of the Word "is distinctly not the handing down of revelation, but it is an indication that revelation is taking place."[25] Or, paraphrasing John Stuart Mill's definition of matter, "the permanent possibility of sensation," we may define the Bible as the permanent possibility of an encounter with God. Thus when the secularized Church of the Middle Ages had, in practice if not in theory, repudiated the Lordship of Christ by substituting herself for her Lord, it was through the Bible that Luther was enabled to establish contact with the Lord of the Church. Confronted by her true Lord, the Church also recovered her true message and her true mission. But in the course of the centuries the Church begotten again by the Word of the Gospel has lost much of the dynamic of the Reformation and has sought to replace the loss by accumulating much of the excess baggage against which the Lord warned His disciples. Protestant theology has found itself in the dilemma of either starving on the empty husks of static intellectualism which its traditional orthodoxy inherited from a decadent scholasticism or else selling its birthright for the pottage of more up-to-date secular science and philosophy. Fundamentalism has followed the former course, modernism the latter. Neither is able to satisfy the reawakened spiritual hunger of our tragic day. Let us, then, observe the need of rediscovering

[25] *Glaube und Erfahrung bei Luther* (1929), p. 119.

the living Word by pointing out: (1) the distress of our age, (2) the breakdown of the traditional orthodoxy, and (3) the failure of its modernistic substitutes.

The distress of the age. The spiritual distress of our day, which leads people of dull conscience to various ways of escaping reality, and people of sensitive conscience to a quest for spiritual guidance, is too obvious to require extended comment. More than one religious leader has applied to the present day Matthew Arnold's description of a generation "wandering between two worlds, one dead, the other powerless to be born." One of the most penetrating of the current statements on the predicament of modern man comes, however, not from a theologian or philosopher but from a political scientist. Professor E. L. Woodward of Oxford University, writing on "The Challenge of Our Time,"[26] gives three grounds for holding that our age is one of special crisis. The first is that the oppression of time and chance is heavier because in our mechanized world people find less relief or consolation in their daily work. In the past labor may have been harsh but it had a familiar rhythm and setting. Today the old binding associations of habit are gone, and our large cities are full of people living as strangers in their very homes and surrounded on all sides by mechanized devices which they have made but cannot control toward desired ends. The second is the prevalence of a more general awareness of the possibility of total calamity. People have never before

---

[26.] *Current Religious Thought*, September, 1946.

faced the threat of such wholesale destruction as an impending atomic war holds. The third is that men today have no ultimate compensation, nothing to set against the tyranny of time and chance and the threat of catastrophe. The Hebrew prophets and St. Augustine lived in a world going to pieces, but through the wreckage they saw the coming of God's Kingdom. Modern men do not know whether there is a Mount Zion or a City of God. The crisis is not only around them but within them. They are confused because they have put their trust in scientific method, the best instrument which the human intellect has devised, but the results obtained by the use of that instrument do not ultimately make sense. Somewhere we have missed the point and are living, as William James once said, like cats and dogs in a library, surrounded by wisdom but unable to grasp its meaning.

Against such a background we appreciate the truth of the assertion made by the late Archbishop of Canterbury, William Temple, "The dominant problem of contemporary religious thought is the problem of revelation."[27] Has the silence of the spheres been broken? Has the distance which sin and ignorance impose between man and his Maker been bridged? Has an authoritative word been spoken which gives ultimate meaning to human existence and solves the riddle of human destiny? Above all, can I in the loneliness and sinfulness of my personal existence hear that word

---

[27.] Baillie and Martin, *Revelation* (N. Y.: Macmillan, 1937), p. 83.

spoken to me, so that doubt will give way to certainty, and isolation to fellowship? This is the perennial and fundamental question of man and to find an answer to it is our most distressing need.

The breakdown of fundamentalism. In the face of this need, traditional orthodoxy, commonly known as fundamentalism, breaks down. This is our second reason for re-emphasizing the living Word proclaimed by Paul and by Luther. According to the fundamentalist view, the Word of God in its central and proper sense is not synonymous with the Christian proclamation, Christ and the Gospel, but with the written documents of the Old and the New Testament now contained in canonical Scripture. Since these documents are held to have been written under the direct and unique guidance of the Holy Spirit, known as "verbal inspiration," they are alleged to be free from any error or discrepancy and to speak infallible divine truth on every matter with which they deal, nonreligious as well as religious. In America this view has been considered to be characteristic of Lutheranism, although, as we have already seen, Luther himself did not hold it, and the leading theologians of the Lutheran countries of Europe today, almost without exception, repudiate it. Historically the roots of this attitude may be traced to the post-Exilic Jewish synagogue. Its resurgence in Protestant Christianity in the period immediately following the Reformation has the same motivation as does its original appearance, namely, the need of the authority of an infallible book to take the place of a shattered institutional authority. Among the Lutherans, however, bibliolatry never reached the proportions it did among the Reformed. The Helvetic Confession of the Swiss Reformed church, for instance, declares divine inspiration to apply to the vowel points of the Hebrew Old Testament, which later scholarship has shown to have been added many centuries after the original writing. The Lutheran Confessions do not bind the conscience of a believer to any theory of inspiration.

The fundamentalists deserve high commendation for their loyalty to the Bible, their appreciation of its worth, and their zeal in defending its central doctrines. As an adherent of the historic Christian Gospel, specifically of confessional Lutheranism, the present writer feels genuine regret in not being able to go all the way with them without compromising his intelligence and his conscience. Furthermore, he is convinced that many who formally subscribe to the theory of verbal inspiration and literal inerrancy, because they have never seriously faced the difficulty involved in holding such a view, actually live by the dynamic concept of the Word. To use Luther's metaphor, if the Bible is the manger in which the Christ-child lies, they do not in reality place such high value upon the manger because it is an absolutely flawless manger, but because it contains Christ. Living Lutheranism is too evangelical and too Christ-centered to yield strict adherence to fundamentalism. Thus the Missouri theologian J. T. Mueller[28] admits that there are small "external" discrepancies even in the unanimously accepted canonical books of the Bible. If we follow the example of Luther, we can afford to pass by the small external discrepancies, since they have nothing to do with the Gospel itself, but the strict fundamentalist cannot afford to do so. Being committed to a theory of absolute textual inerrancy, he is disturbed by the possibility of even the slightest error, and when such a possibility is suggested, he is compelled to turn aside from the Gospel to devise means of defending his theory at all costs. Much ingenuity has been wasted in seeking to reconcile, for example, the account of Paul's conversion experience in Acts 9:1–9, according to which his companions on the road to Damascus *heard* a voice but *saw* nothing, with the account in Acts 22:6–11, according to which they *saw* the light but *heard* nothing. Likewise, to use but one other example, only those already committed to verbal inspiration are satisfied with the attempts to harmonize Paul's reference in I Corinthians 10:8 to 23,000 Israelites killed at Shittim, with the original figure of 24,000 given in Numbers 25:9. When one's preconception does not allow him to accept any such natural explanation as a possible slip in Paul's memory, he is forced to escape the facts at hand by conjecturing that Paul had access to esoteric information about the Old Testament, which we do not possess, or by insisting

---

[28.] *Christian Dogmatics*, p. 111.

that the Holy Spirit has a right to revise His own statements. The usual escape, however, is to retreat from the
area of combat on the wings of the fanciful hypothesis
of the errorlessness of the original documents of the
Bible. Since these documents are irrevocably lost, and
no one can ever prove or disprove what is in them, the
fundamentalist flight ends in a Shangri-la of sheer
speculation where logical thinking cannot follow. Such
a solution places a much greater strain on credibility
than a simple and frank admission that God used nor-
mal fallible human beings in revealing Himself to us.

That the fundamentalist approach cannot meet a
thinking modern man's need for God is clear. It will
still win assent among the unthinking, for the original
assertion of errorlessness, if made emphatically enough
and often enough, may be accepted without challenge
and there will be no reason to expose the vulnerability
of the supporting hypothesis. With thinking people
fundamentalism does more harm than good, for it dis-
torts the true function of the Bible by distracting attention from the divine treasure to the earthen vessel.
When the human side of the Bible has been vested with
the authority of divine inerrancy, and its true nature
becomes manifest, this tragic result is likely to follow:
the ways in which the biblical writers were human
beings like the rest of us, and children of their time,
will triumph over the ways in which they are witnesses
to God's eternal and saving truth. From the point of
view of the living Word, Christ and His Gospel, the

case against fundamentalism may be summed up in three propositions.

First, fundamentalism is incompatible with the Bible's own vital method of self-authentication. Heaping extravagant praise on the book and claiming miraculous origin for it does not place the Bible in a different category from the Koran or the Book of Mormon. Mere appeal to the authority of the Bible proves no point, for every sectarian and fanatic quotes Scripture to support his position. With all its well-meant loyalty to the Bible, fundamentalistic biblicism must bear a heavy responsibility for the scandal of Protestantism, the splitting of the Church into hundreds of fragments, each claiming to be more scriptural than the other. The futility of defending the Bible by vehement argument, as well as the true way, was clearly seen by Calvin: "Though anyone vindicates the sacred word of God from the aspersions of men, yet this will not fix in their hearts that assurance which is essential to true piety."[29] Such assurance does not come through any theory of inspiration but only through the "Gospel of God concerning His Son" appropriated in personal faith. This Gospel needs only release, not defense. It provides its own dynamic vindication. The Bible, like the Holy Spirit who inspired it, does not testify of itself but of Christ. It is only when spiritual fires are burning low that men attach primary importance to the Bible rather than to its living content, Christ.

---

[29] *Inst.*, I, 7, 4.

Second, fundamentalism is incompatible with the method of divine revelation in general. God's revelation of Himself is marked throughout by a bipolarity of the human and the divine. When God made the supreme and final revelation of Himself, He sent forth His Son, under the form of a servant, clothed in genuine human flesh. The Church rejected the docetic heresy which so glorified the divine nature of Christ that it reduced His human nature to an empty shadow. When Christ established His Church to be the continuation of His incarnation, it too came to have two natures, the human nature of a historical institution and the divine nature of the Kingdom of God on earth. The Church rejects as heresy the claim of Rome to transcend human fallibility and to be the divine authority itself. And when Christ gave His Church the sacrament by which His real presence was to be experienced through the ages, He used the earthly elements of bread and wine, which were to be received in a thoroughly human manner. The Church rejects as heretical the magic of transubstantiation whereby bread and wine lose their real substance and are changed into the body and blood of Christ. Why, then, should we presume that God's revelation of Himself in Scripture should differ from this basic design? Is not the deification of the Bible into something divinely inerrant a form of the docetic heresy, a denial of the human nature of the Word? Does not the infallible Bible of fundamentalism belong in the same category as the infallible pope of Roman Cathol-

icism, indicating a transfer of Christ's own authority
to a representative in history? Is not therefore Luther's
appeal from the Bible to Christ, the King of the Bible,
a profound evangelical insight? And finally, does not
Christ give Himself to us "in, with, and under" a human
word in Scripture as He does "in, with, and under" the
visible elements in the sacrament? Is not the attempt
to change the human and fallible in the sacred writers
into something divine and infallible of a piece with the
magic of transubstantiation? Is it any more reasonable
to demand flawlessness in the medium of written communication than to demand an absolutely flawless communion wafer? The historical fact is that it has pleased
God to deny errorlessness to the documents by which
His Word actually has reached us. Thus even in the
Scriptures He has so concealed Himself behind an unpretentious exterior that only faith can say: the Scriptures are the Word of God. Here too we have been
given not a "theology of glory" but a "theology of the
Cross." In the words of Emil Brunner, "The characteristic 'style' of God's revelation is to avail itself of the
form of a servant, to humiliate itself deeply and suffer
descent into earthly frailties, not to thrust itself on
men's view with the pomp of heathen theophanies but
even in the act of revelation to let itself be sought for
as something hidden. It is in keeping with God's choice
of a small, insignificant, and uncouth people, and with
His revelation of His profoundest mystery on the cross
at Golgotha that He gave us His Word in a literary

document which will give the critics, in the legitimate exercise of their task, enough to do for generations to come."[30]

Third and last, fundamentalism must yield to the living Word because it is incompatible with the mission of the Holy Spirit to teach us new truth. Such is the static rationalism in the attitude of traditional Protestant scholasticism that it approaches Scripture itself with a purpose of seeking corroboration and proof for its own doctrines rather than with a mind open and receptive to the Spirit who has been given to guide us into all truth. If we consider the Bible as primarily a fixed body of doctrines, then we may presume to know its content from previous study, before we study and interpret it afresh. The Bible thus turns out to be little more than a collection of proof-texts. God has spoken in the past but He no longer speaks. Inspiration has been frozen to a fixed period in past history. Just as the Roman Catholics have their dogma of immaculate conception, a dogma of supernatural origin, to support their Mariolatry, so fundamentalistic Protestants have their verbal inspiration, a dogma of the miraculous supernatural origin of the Bible. Both have reference to a dead past. The living Word, on the other hand, depends on the constant faith-creating activity of the Spirit who through the record of past revelation speaks a fresh personal word to each individual willing to listen. Unaccompanied by the witness of the Spirit, the Bible remains a dead let-

---

[30] *The Philosophy of Religion* (New York: Scribner's, 1937), p. 156.

ter. The Word of God in its true sense is present only where the response of faith occurs, just as no sound occurs when no ear is present to hear it.

The failure of modernism. If traditional intellectualistic orthodoxy is inadequate to the task of confronting modern man with God's living Word, the failure of its liberalistic substitutes is still more obvious. In the words of Karl Barth, "Modernist thought hears man answer without anyone having called him. It hears him talk to himself."[31] Either it makes a god of some philosophical or scientific abstraction, a dumb idol powerless to speak, or else it is out-and-out atheism. The latest phase of American liberal theology is strikingly represented by one of its foremost spokesmen, Henry Nelson Wieman, whose latest book *The Source of Human Good* attempts to "show the mythical nature of two deep-laid Christian teachings, the transcendental status and the personal character of God." Wieman's substitute for the Creator is an impersonal principle of creativity manifest, among other things, in the procreative process. This degenerate theology has drawn a deserved rebuke from Dr. Charles Clayton Morrison. Just as "behavioristic psychology cuts off man's head—his manhood—and leaves him only a truncated body of behavior activities," he writes, "Wieman cuts off God's head--his Godhead—and gives us a truncated God which is only a behavior process of creative activity." Such behavioristic theology, he concludes, "should open the eyes of Christian

---

[31] *Op. cit.,* p. 68.

teachers and leaders to discern where the true enemy, not only of Christian faith, but of Western culture itself, is located."[32]

The same conclusion may be applied to America's most famous living philosopher, John Dewey, who in a recent symposium entitled *Naturalism and the Human Spirit* reaffirms his profession to know nothing of any resources except those drawn from the natural environment. Impatient with those who have pointed out the debt which his own type of scientific and democratic thought owes to the Christian heritage, Dewey explicitly disowns that heritage. In the same volume his disciple J. H. Randall, Jr., declares: "There is no room for any Supernatural in naturalism—no supernatural or transcendental God and no personal survival after death."[33] Another essayist in the symposium, Sterling P. Lamprecht, questions the propriety of such a warping of language as the use of the word "God" when the being to which the established usage refers is no longer believed to exist. And since the existence of God cannot be demonstrated, Professor Lamprecht cautions against taking religion too seriously. It should be taken, he says, with a light touch and a sense of humor, not as something authoritative for all of life but only experimental for certain parts of it. These philosophers at least, unlike the Christian liberals who follow such lead-

[32] *The Christian Century*, Nov. 13, 1946, pp. 1375-76.

[33] *Naturalism and the Human Spirit*, ed. Y. H. Krikorian (New York: Columbia University Press, 1944), p. 358.

ership, arrive honestly at their atheistic conclusions and do not try to camouflage them under pious verbiage. Dewey is indeed to be commended for defining clearly the basic issue and thus showing the untenability of any theology which relies on non-Christian resources. The issue, he points out, is between a thorough naturalism and a thorough supernaturalism, while an idealism which seeks to mediate between them is "the diluted philosophic version of historic supernaturalism,"[34] Much of our current and supposedly "advanced" religious philosophizing, in pulpits as well as in books and classrooms, is still unaware of this fundamental issue and persists in spreading confusion by offering synthetic substitutes for the Word of God. Many a modernistic discourse could be aptly characterized by the comment which Charles Reynolds Brown, while professor of homiletics at Yale, wrote on the manuscript of a student sermon: "It is without form and void; darkness is on the face of it."

Although the scientific philosophers of our day arrive logically at their atheistic conclusion, there is nothing new either in the fundamental procedure or in the result. Paul drew the same inference nineteen centuries ago: "The world did not know God through wisdom" (I Cor. 1:21). But Paul had more to say. He had been overpowered by a "wisdom of God" which was also the "power of God." It radiated from Christ the Crucified, and while it had the appearance of foolishness and

---

[34] *Ibid.,* p. 9.

weakness and scandalized the philosophers, it pleased God through this apparent folly to disclose Himself in His saving power to those who responded to it with their whole lives. This is the "living Word" of the Apostles and of the Reformers, and it is the Word which alone can make God real to modern men.

It remains for us to summarize in conclusion what it means to us to rediscover this stream of living truth as over against a traditionalism which would freeze it and a liberalism which would evaporate it. It means, first, that God has not only spoken in the past and caused His Word to be reduced to writing, but He still speaks today. As Archbishop Söderblom expressed it, "The chief lesson of the Bible itself is that God is a living God and has not grown aged or less active now than in His younger days."[35] It means, second, that God speaks to you and to me personally in the concrete life-situations in which we are. His Word does not bear the general heading "To whom it may concern"; it is addressed to me by name. The important thing is not my interest in what is called "religion" but God's interest in me. Just as Christ once called Peter on the lakeside, Matthew at the revenue office, and Paul on the Damascus road, so as the living Lord of history, our eternal contemporary, He confronts me. I have not had my rendezvous with destiny until my life has come before His judgment and His mercy, until I have responded to

[35] *Nature of Revelation* (N. Y.: Oxford Univ. Press, 1933), p. 179.

Him, either in repudiation or commitment. The living
Word means, third, that the Word which God speaks
to me is a redeeming Word. It says, "I have called thee
by name," in order to say, "I have redeemed thee." It
is Christ bringing to me His Gospel and new life for
me in God. As Bishop Brilioth of Sweden has recently
expressed it, the Word comes so frightfully close to me,
because it is not content with telling me about sacred
history in the past but is bent upon transforming my
life into a chapter of sacred history.[36] The living Word
comes to me, fourth, through the agency which it has
itself created, through the Church, the Body of Christ
and His continuing incarnation, specifically through its
proclamation, its sacred writings, its sacraments, its fellowship. Those of us who are ministers of the Church
and servants of the Word have been entrusted with
these resources for no less a purpose than to bring men
face to face with Christ himself. It is not enough for
us to explain the parable of the dragnet; we have been
called to be fishers of men, to cast out the dragnet and
draw men into the Kingdom. We have not done our
duty when we have given the correct interpretation of
the invitation to the wedding of the King's son; we have
been commissioned to invite men to the royal wedding.
Only a living Church can be the carrier of the living
Word. Finally, the Word reveals its living content only
to the eyes of faith. Where men have trusted God with

[36] H. S. Nyberg, A. Fridrichsen, Y. Brilioth, *Bibelns enhet* (Stock-
holm, 1945), chap. 3.

all their heart, God has revealed to them His own heart. Faith, as Paul Tillich has said, "is the revolutionary act in which God gives Himself to us, person to person."[37] Where there is no such divine self-giving and self-disclosure, it is foolish presumption to speak at all about a supernatural reality which remains utterly beyond the reach of all scientific method, to say nothing of pretending to have intimate knowledge of such a reality, as one person has of another. Men can speak a meaningful word *about* God or *for* God only when in faith they have actually heard the Word *of* God and responded *to* God. Thus and thus alone is the silence imposed by both science and the reticence of common sense broken. "I believe, therefore I speak."

The concept of the Word we have thus obtained is something much more than a body of correct propositions or flawless words. The Word is not only the revealer of divine wisdom but also and primarily the vehicle of divine power, the power to give vital conviction, to break sinful habit, to redirect the will, to bridge the chasm between God and man. When this dynamic view of the Word is grasped, a radically new appraisal of the function and worth of Scripture follows. It will then appear to be faint praise to describe the Bible as "the golden casket where gems of truth are stored" or "the chart and compass" which guides the seeker after truth to Christ. Such static imagery, involving man as the active agent who discovers divine

---

[37.] *Christendom,* VII (1943), 524.

truth and uses it as an instrument of guidance, will give way to an appreciation of Scripture as genuine means of grace by which God seeks man, speaks to him, gives him new life in fellowship. Much of the time-honored controversy concerning the Bible, the correctness of its scientific views and the mode of its inspiration, will be seen to be quite beside the point. We shall recapture the original lifegiving dynamism of our Scriptures and our Confessions: "Through the Word and the Sacraments, as through instruments, the Holy Ghost is given, who worketh faith where and when it pleaseth God in them that hear the Gospel" (Article V, Augsburg Confession). "For as the rain cometh down and the snow from heaven, and returneth not thither, but watereth the earth and maketh it bring forth and bud, that it may give seed to the sower and bread to the eater: so shall my Word be that goeth forth out of my mouth: it shall not return unto me void, but it shall accomplish that which I please, and it shall prosper in the thing whereto I sent it" (Isa. 55:10-11).

CHAPTER IV

UNIVERSAL SPIRITUAL PRIESTHOOD
AND LIFE IN SOCIETY

GROWING OUT of the grace which justifies sinful man
and restores him to a right relationship to God and man,
and out of the living Word, by which that restoration
is effected, is the third of the foundation-principles of
evangelical theology, the spiritual priesthood of all believers. It represents the life of faith in action and is
thus the specific ethical and social principle of the Gospel. The underlying motivation of all Christian action,
of course, is love, but love in its proper Christian connotation is not human activity at all. It is but another
name for grace, God's own redeeming action which
reconstructs human personalities to be its working tools.
Christian love is not the moral effort of man either to
do good or to repay God for His goodness. As Nygrén
has shown, it flows spontaneously from its own source,
the God who is Love, wherever a right relation to God
exists. But if we observe the God-motivated life from
the human point of view of being "constrained by the
love of Christ," of being under an overpowering inner
compulsion to say, "Love so amazing, so divine, de-

mands my soul, my life, my all," then it is best described as the consecrated life, the life of priesthood. The scope of this priesthood, as well as its nature and function, is determined by its source. It is as universal and free from stratification as the divine love which calls it into being. According to the Lord's own teaching in the Sermon on the Mount, it operates with the same disregard of fences of all kinds as rain and sunshine. Nor does it mean that since each man is his own priest, free from ecclesiastical tyranny, he is therefore also free from social responsibility. On the contrary, to have free access to God as a child to his father means to be liberated and empowered for a service of love to the whole family of God's children. To be a priest is essentially to be consecrated to serve. When the love of God in Christ has taken a man off his own hands, then, in the words of Nels Ferré, "the will to live has become a will to love; the will to power, a will to fellowship; the will to superiority, a will to service; the will to social recognition, a will to social responsibility and concern."[1] Universal spiritual priesthood thus has tremendous implications not only for personal sanctification but also for the Christian fellowship and for the extension of its transforming influence into all areas of life. Let us study this exceedingly rich and dynamic principle, as we have studied the other two basic principles of our theology, sketching first its scriptural and historical background and then restating its meaning for our day.

---

[1] *Return to Christianity* (New York: Harper, 1943), p. 17.

I. SCRIPTURAL AND HISTORICAL BACKGROUND

The priesthood of all Christian believers is explicitly set forth in I Peter 2:5, 9 and Revelation 1:5-6, 5:9-10, and 20:6. If the scriptural foundation for the principle appears to be slight, two considerations must be borne in mind. First, these passages are the only ones in the New Testament in which Christian priesthood is at all mentioned; all other references to priests or priesthood are either to the priestly office of Christ or to Jewish and pagan priests. Second, the thought underlying the principle is so richly supported in other forms of speech both by the teaching of Christ himself and by the proclamation and practice of the apostolic church that its validity cannot be questioned nor its importance overestimated.

Before turning to the latter consideration, let us call to mind the specific *sedes doctrinae*. The passages in I Peter 2 are: "Like living stones be yourselves built into a spiritual house, to be a holy priesthood, to offer spiritual sacrifices acceptable to God through Jesus Christ" and "But you are a chosen race, a royal priesthood, a holy nation, God's own people, that you may declare the wonderful deeds of him who called you out of darkness into his marvelous light." Here the apostolic church appropriates for itself the status of *qahal Jahve*, the assembly of Israel, God's chosen people, the holy remnant of a nation which had defaulted its destiny by spurning the Messiah. As the true people of the Messiah the Christians constitute a royal and consecrated nation in which every member shares in the Messiah's kingly, priestly, and prophetic mission. He not only enjoys a high spiritual status and a free access to God mediated only by Christ, but he is also called to bear witness to God's wonderful deeds, so that they who are still in the darkness may also come to share the marvelous light of the Kingdom. It is important to observe that the term *laos,* translated *people,* which is used here, is the source of our words *laity* and *layman.* Subsequent corruption of the apostolic doctrine has led to the view that laymen are on a lower spiritual level than priests. In the New Testament, to be a member of the laity, of Christ's people, is to be a member of a royal priesthood. It is such a high standing in its own God-given right that no office held within the universal priesthood can rank above it. To be a Christian is therefore infinitely more important than to be a clergyman, an archbishop, or a pope. Beside the all-important distinction of being "in Christ" or "out of Christ," distinctions within the Christian fellowship are dwarfed into relative insignificance.

The three statements in the Book of Revelation which refer to universal spiritual priesthood are: "To him who loves us and has freed us from our sins by his blood and made us a kingdom, priests to his God and Father, to him be glory and dominion for ever and ever"; "Worthy art thou to take the scroll and to open its seals, for thou wast slain and by thy blood didst ransom men for God, from every tribe and tongue and people and nation, and hast made them a kingdom and priests to our God and they shall reign on earth"; "But they shall be priests of God and of Christ, and they shall reign with him a thousand years." Quite aside from the mooted question of the interpretation of the millennial kingdom, to which the last statement refers, the unequivocal teaching of all these passages is that Christians constitute a holy community and that Christ, the head of this community, has given to each member of it a status and a mission which must be described by the messianic terms of kingly and priestly. Particularly significant is the basic evangelical emphasis that Christians owe their high calling not to their own worthiness but solely to the redeeming love of the crucified Lamb of God who transforms slaves and paupers into kings and priests. The vital relation between justifying grace and universal priesthood is nowhere more impressively expressed. The faith of the martyrs voiced by the Book of Revelation is faith in "the blood of the Lamb" but it also empowers them to shed their own blood in heroic witness to this faith.

This conception of Christian discipleship as membership in a divinely ordained community, every member of which is consecrated to a royal mission, is richly supported by the rest of the New Testament. It stems, in fact, from the heart of our Lord's own message, the proclamation of the Kingdom of God. "He made us into a Kingdom" is a necessary consequence of Jesus' messiahship, for there can be no messiah without a messianic people. Whether within that people He established any specific form of organization or gradations of office will remain subject to endless debate. But there can be no question about the call to sacred service which He issued to all His people nor about the kingly resources which He placed at their disposal for this purpose. Whenever He spoke in lofty terms about himself and His messianic vocation, He proceeded forthwith to speak in the same lofty terms about His people and their vocation. Did he say, "I am the light of the world"? Yes, but He also said, "You are the light of the world." Did He say that He performed mighty works, which should lead people to trust Him? Yes, but He also said, "Greater works than these shall he (the believer) do." Did He say that the Father had sent Him into the world to carry out a great mission? Yes, but He also said, "As the Father has sent me, even so I send you." And when His own historical mission was completed, He actually did entrust the entire work of the Kingdom on earth to His people: "Go into all the world and preach the Gospel to the whole creation." "Go and make disciples of all nations." This is an enterprise of such tremendous proportions that it is simply unthinkable without the participation of the entire membership of the Christian community. But even the most concerted action on the part of all Christians would still be inadequate. "Without me," says Christ, "you can do nothing." The greatest asset of the messianic people in carrying out their messianic mission is the Messiah himself. "I am with you always."

To have membership in the messianic people meant also to have high responsibilities with reference to personal conduct and to life within the fellowship. It is in this light that the exceedingly lofty ethical and social standards of the Sermon on the Mount are to be interpreted. Others may be governed by conformity to tradition or to what men may rationally expect, but not so the people of the Messiah. Their standard is nothing less than God's own perfection. They are therefore to live so far above the average as to exceed the righteousness of even those paragons of respectability, the scribes and the Pharisees. The criterion, as well as the dynamic, for great living is whether one is in or out of the Kingdom. Even the least in the Kingdom is greater than the greatest in any other sphere. In the Kingdom the relations between man and man and between man and woman are judged by reference not to legal statutes but to the absolute will of God. The entire juridic point of view, the desire to be fair and to fit the punishment to the offense, is supplanted by the point of view of love, the desire to redeem. While the non-Kingdom man evaluates in terms of power to lord it over others, the Kingdom man, using the example of his Lord who came "not to be served but to serve," measures greatness by service. And in the last judgment God himself will decide man's final destiny on the basis of self-forgetting works of love.

This service of love need not be religious in any professional sense. One revenue collector, Matthew, is

called to be an apostle, but another, Zacchaeus, is returned to his office to carry on the old business but with
a new attitude. Hereafter that post will be manned by
one working for a higher realm than the Roman Empire.
Nor does membership in the Kingdom lead necessarily
to any direct effort to overthrow or change the existing
order. The tax dollar must be paid to Caesar, even
though it contributes to the support of an unjust and
ruthless political order. The people of God can confidently leave to Him the ultimate questions of how and
when the kingdoms of this world will become the kingdoms of God and His Messiah. It has pleased God to
have given them the Kingdom already, and it is for
them to be found faithful to it whatever their worldly
position may be. But their Lord will continue not only
to awaken kingly thoughts even in peasant hearts but
also to make even the simplest act performed in loyalty
to Him, such as the handing of a cup of water to one
who thirsts, an act of royal dignity and sacred worship.

In the writings of Paul we are confronted with the
same approach to Christian life and work in terms of
the high calling which every believer has "in Christ"
and in the fellowship of His people, and the tremendous
responsibilities and resources which this status brings.
Paul too describes the Christian community as the messianic nation, "the Israel of God" (Gal. 6:16), "Abra-
ham's offspring, heirs according to promise" (Gal.
3:29), "the true circumcision" (Phil. 3:3), "heirs of
God and fellow-heirs with Christ" (Rom. 8:17). In the

most impressive and vivid of his metaphors, the Apostle portrays the Church as "the body of Christ" into which every believer becomes incorporated through baptism. Within this organism are various offices, just as in the physical body there are various functions performed by the constituent organs, but there are no distinctions of rank. And unless each member carries out his function, the whole organism suffers. Indeed, the members apparently lacking in honor and ostentation may perform the most indispensable functions. The "more excellent way" by which each specific action best finds its goal is love (*agape*), the glowing praise of which, in I Corinthians 13, significantly enough grows out of this context. When we remember that for Paul the fountain from which love flows is the Cross where Christ died for us while we were yet sinners, we appreciate the vital connection between Christian action and the center of Paul's proclamation, the grace which justifies and sanctifies. Those who are thus "consecrated in Christ Jesus" are "called to be saints together with all those who in every place call on the name of our Lord Jesus Christ" (I Cor. 1:2).

The usual Pauline designation for the members of the universal spiritual priesthood is the term "saints." This word characterizes at once their relationship to their Lord, who has called them from the sinful life of the world and consecrates them to be His people; to each other, in the sacred fellowship of shared joy, suffering, and burden-bearing; and to the world, to which they are "letters from Christ." Their conduct, therefore, should be such "as is fitting among saints," so that the sins of impurity and covetousness, common among those who are not "in Christ," should not even be mentioned among them (Eph. 5:3). But the exercise of saintliness does not mean a monastic withdrawal from ordinary life. The people of God, like other people, are to live within the orders of creation, but they are to bring into these orders the transforming power of the new order of redemption to which they belong. Thus *agape* furnishes the atmosphere for the Christian home, and Christ's relation to the Church the spiritual ideal for the husband-wife relationship. The Christian spirit invests the economic order likewise with a God-given dignity. It is "in the Lord Jesus Christ" that Paul exhorts men "to earn their own living" by honest work, according to the principle "If any man will not work, let him not eat" (II Thess. 3:10-12). Work enables a man not only to make a living but also to maintain self-respect and to be in position to serve others (I Thess. 4:11-12, Eph. 4:28). And to the political order the Christian brings a high sense of civic responsibility as a God-given duty. He is obedient and loyal to political authority as to a power ordained of God. Like his Lord, Paul was no political or social rebel. Thus while "in Christ" there is neither slave nor free (Gal. 3:28), he did not agitate against slavery but admonished slaves, upon becoming Christians, to remain slaves (I Cor. 7:20-23). Paul knew that the

Roman Empire, where there were ten times as many slaves as freemen, rested upon slavery, and that abolition would have meant revolution. He had been commissioned to preach Christ, not to promote political revolution. But he was also confident, as in the case of Onesimus and Philemon, that Christian love would bring about spiritual equality and mutual understanding between slave and master, and that here lay the power for solving the whole problem in an ever widening scope. It is the love which "bears all things" which also dares to "hope all things." As a summary of Paul's message to the communion of saints we may take his word of vision and assurance of ultimate triumph: "All things are yours . . . and you are Christ's, and Christ is God's" (I Cor. 3:21-23).

In the primitive Christian church universal spiritual priesthood was more than a doctrine rooted in the messianic mission of Christ and taught by Peter, John, and Paul. It was the living force which enabled Christianity to get a foothold in the ancient world, to spread, and to triumph over the fiercest kind of opposition. "They went forth and preached everywhere, while the Lord worked with them" (Mark 16:20). This is a description of all Christians, not only of the apostles. In fact, when persecution struck the Church in Jerusalem, Luke tells us, "they were all scattered . . . except the apostles," and "those who were scattered went about preaching the word" (Acts 8:1-4). Historians, secular as well as theological, are generally agreed that primitive Christianity was primarily a "lay movement" whose chief instrument of propagation was the witness, through life and word, of the rank and file of Christians. "It became the most sacred duty of a new convert," says Gibbon, "to diffuse among his friends and relations the inestimable blessing which he had received."[2] Every Christian, whether he was a merchant or soldier or slave, became a missionary. According to Adolf Harnack, "We cannot hesitate to believe that the great mission of Christianity was in reality accomplished by means of informal missionaries."[3] And T. R. Glover shows just how these informal missionaries achieved their success: "The real conviction of the living Christ was not carried to the world by a book nor by a story. Men might allege they had seen the risen Lord; that was nothing till they themselves were known. The witness of the Resurrection was not the word of Paul . . . nor of the eleven; it was the new power in life and death that the world saw in changed men. . . . The legend of a reputed resurrection of some unknown person in Palestine nobody needed to consider, but what were you to do with the people who died in the arena, the reborn slaves with their newness of life in your own house? . . . The conviction of the people you knew, amazing in its power of transforming character and

<hr>

[2] Edward Gibbon, *The History of the Decline and Fall of the Roman Empire* (London: Methuen, 1896), II, 7.

[3] Adolf Harnack, *The Expansion of Christianity in the First Three Centuries* (New York: Putnam, 1904), I, 460.

winning first the good will and the trust and then the conversion of others, was supported and confirmed by the nature and personality of the Man of whom they spoke, of whom you read in their books."[4] Glover cites as typical the case of Tertullian, a lawyer and a Stoic philosopher who became an influential church father. Tertullian was not led to Christ by the Scriptures: "Nobody comes to them," he writes, "unless he is already a Christian." He became a Christian when he began to inquire into the source of the courage manifested by the Christians he saw being martyred in the Roman amphitheatre. If the blood of the martyrs was not the seed of the Church, it was at least the agency by which hard ground was softened and prepared to receive the seed, the Word of God.

When the age of the martyrs was over and the Church received official recognition and favor in the empire, a period of rapid expansion and consolidation ensued. But the Church paid an exceedingly high price for its worldly success and prestige. The functions of the universal spiritual priesthood were gradually usurped by a hierarchical organization based upon non-apostolic distinctions of rank. Priesthood became identified with a professional religious order, mediating between God and ordinary Christians, and the latter were relegated to a more and more passive and inferior role, amounting in many cases to little more than nom-

---

[4] T. R. Glover, *The Influence of Christ in the Ancient World* (Cambridge: University Press, 1929), pp. 96 ff.

inal membership in an ecclesiastical institution. A definite substitution of a sacerdotal hierarchy of bishops for the priesthood of all believers can be found already in the teaching of the ante-Nicene Father, St. Cyprian. By the time of Pope Gregory VII in the eleventh century the royal priesthood of the apostolic age had been transformed into an ecclesiastical theocracy with the pope at its head. Impersonal mass methods had taken the place of person-to-person witnessing as the instrument for propagating the faith. The communion of saints had become a stratified society in which merits were transferred from one class to another according to fixed institutional regulations. Least meritorious were the deeds performed by ordinary people at home and at work. The Church thus deprived the common life of its sanctity, and placed a halo upon religious mendicancy and parasitism. It has been estimated that when Luther began the Reformation, only one person in fifteen in Germany worked for a living. Even the lay orders which through the Middle Ages had kept alive a practical applied Christianity had become dead weight which impeded true social progress.

One of the most important aspects in the life work of Luther is that in rediscovering the Gospel he rediscovered also the Gospel's own vital method for releasing its power into the common life of humanity. To the great Reformer, affirms John R. Mott, "more largely than to any other man, the world is indebted for the rescue and reassertion of the principle of the priesthood of all believers."[5] To Luther universal spiritual priesthood was much more than a weapon with which to attack the Roman hierarchy. It was the fundamental principle of the entire evangelical outlook, growing directly out of the Gospel itself and bearing fruit in all areas of human life. As such it is clearly anticipated in Luther's lectures on the Psalms and on Romans before the open break with Rome, and it comes to full expression in the early reformatory writings. In the *Address to the Christian Nobility* it is the first of the trumpet-blasts by which the walls of Rome are to be demolished. "Priests, bishops or popes . . . are neither different from other Christians nor superior to them, except that they are charged with the administration of the Word of God and the sacraments."[6] This is "their work and office," just as shoemakers, blacksmiths, and farmers have their work to do while belonging to the priesthood common to all. In the *Babylonian Captivity of the Church* Luther declares: "As many of us as have been baptized are all priests without distinction" and "Let everyone, therefore, who knows himself to be a Christian be assured of this, and apply it to himself, that we are all priests, and there is no difference between us, that is to say, we have the same power in respect to the Word and all the sacraments."[7]   In replying to Emser, he points out clearly that the ecclesiastical conception of priesthood is a

---

[5.] *Liberating the Lay Forces of Christianity* (New York: Macmillan, 1932), pp. 10-11.

[6.] *Works* (Holman ed.), II, 69.

[7.] *Ibid.,* II, 279, 282.

historical development without foundation in the Scriptures. "If tonsures, consecrations, ointments, vestments, made priests and bishops, then Christ and His apostles were never priests or bishops."[8]

But it is in the treatise on *Christian Liberty* that spiritual priesthood finds its most beautiful expression, especially in its positive ethical and social aspects. Christ makes us not only kings and therefore the most free of all men, but also priests and therefore the most obligated to serve others. Hence "the good things which we have from God ought to flow from one to another, and become common to all, so that every one of us may, as it were, put on his neighbor, and so behave towards him as if he were himself in his place."[9] And rising to the loftiest heights of all, the Reformer resolves: "I will therefore give myself, as a sort of Christ, to my neighbor, as Christ has given Himself to me, and will do nothing in this life except what I see will be needful, advantageous, and wholesome for my neighbor, since by faith I abound in all good things in Christ. . . . And as our heavenly Father has freely helped us in Christ, so ought we freely to help our neighbor by our body and works, and each should become to the other a sort of Christ, so that we may be mutually Christ's, and that the same Christ may be in all of us, that is, that we may be truly Christians."[10] Nowhere in all the fourscore

---

[8] *Ibid.*, III, 324.

[9] *Primary Works,* ed. H. Wace and C. A. Buchheim (London: Hodder and Stoughton, 1896), p. 286.

[10] *Ibid.*, pp. 282-83.

huge volumes of Luther's collected works do we find a
more glorious or dynamic description of what it means
to be a Christian. Yet this side of Luther's teaching has
been almost forgotten. Even Spener, who a century and
a half later revived the emphasis on universal spiritual
priesthood to counteract a lifeless orthodoxy, interpreted it largely in terms of the right of the individual
to pray and to study the Word and had little to say
about service to others. Let us, then, give more specific
attention to the Reformer's teaching on the operation
of this basic principle of the Christian life within the
orders of communal living: the church, the home, and
the political and economic orders.

First of all, universal spiritual priesthood is for Luther
the essence of the Church. The Church is the fellowship
created by the Word and characterized by the Word,
whether read, preached, or sacramentally acted. "God's
Word," declared Luther, "cannot be present without
God's people, and God's people cannot be without God's
Word."[11] But the fellowship of God's people is the
apostolic "communion of saints," the royal priesthood
of all believers, not a sacerdotal institution. As the
product of the Word, the Church belongs to the realm
of faith, and no definite earthly boundaries can be
drawn around it. The Church is therefore not identical
with the Church of Rome nor any other visible organization. Although the world and the crowd reject the
Word and remain unchristian, the Word does not return

---

[11] *Works* (Holman ed.), V, 270 ff.

void. Wherever it is present, in any of its forms, even
in Rome, it generates faith and unites believers with
the invisible Body of Christ. From the point of view of
love we may think of it as co-extensive with the number
of baptized persons, but from the point of view of faith
we can acknowledge as its members only the justified
and the elect, i.e., those in whom God's redeeming purpose comes to fulfillment. But we cannot presume to
draw the line between true and false members lest we
pull up the wheat with the tares. At all events, the
Church is rooted in God's own eternal purpose, not in
any accident of history, and may be identified with
God's Kingdom on earth. It existed as "the true Israel"
already before the birth of Christ and will continue
until Christ turns over His sovereignty to the Father,
and God is all in all. During its mission on earth, however, the Church, like its Lord, manifests both a human
and a divine nature. The preaching of the Word and
the administration of the sacraments give the Church
its visibility and require an institutional organization.
As a historical institution the Church is subject to limitations and shortcomings, and may be described, just
as the individual believer, as "simul iustus et peccator."
No primary importance attaches to any specific form of
organization. Luther was willing to accept even the
papacy with its obvious weaknesses if only the Word
of God had been given a free course. The visible organization, however, has ceased to be the Christian Church
when it has exchanged the ministry of the Word for a

Levitical priesthood offering sacrifices, making atonement, mediating salvation. The Christian ministry is a representative office, not a vicarial order. The prerogatives of the universal spiritual priesthood are never transferred to the ministry, but through the ministry, entrusted to properly qualified and called representatives, these prerogatives come into rightly ordered exercise. The acts which the minister performs in proclaiming the Word and administering the sacraments are not his own but those of the Church. He has no "indelible character," and when he ceases to preach the Word he ceases to be a minister.

The priesthood of all believers determines not only the structure and function of the Church but also the life within the Church. In the medieval church, with its striving for merit in order to gain salvation, Luther saw the substitution of a kind of consecrated selfishness for the true Christian motivation of love. In the church which draws its life from the Gospel of grace Christian love comes into its own. We do not perform acts of kindness in order to become Christians but because God has already, out of pure love, made us Christians. In true Christian activity service to needy living saints takes the place of veneration of dead ones. Luther's conception of membership in the Church is remarkably rich and vital. Since Christ bears our own burdens, we are free to bear the burdens of the brethren. Each Christian is a spiritual priest to whom a fellow-Christian may unburden his soul, and who as a sort of Christ or mediator will carry the other's load of guilt. In such a community whatever one has belongs to the others. Were it not for the fact that in order to give one must have, Luther would have abolished private property altogether within the evangelical congregations. But he insisted that possessions exist only as means of service. In the communion of saints mutual sharing, economic as well as spiritual, is so thorough that one becomes "baked" together with Christ and His people into one "bread."[12] A Christian is therefore never alone. Whatever difficulty or suffering he must face, Christ and all the saints are at his side. Since love is the motivating power of the Christian fellowship, Luther rejects the medieval doctrine of the two swords, one borne by the state, the other by the Church. The Church has no sword, but only the Word, and coercive measures are foreign to its spirit.

Spiritual priesthood is the key not only to Luther's doctrine of the Church but also to his conception of Christian responsibility in the orders of secular life. In the sphere of marriage and home it enables him to be as important a reformer as in the Church. Revolting against the inconsistencies and the hypocrisies of the sacramentarian view of marriage and priestly celibacy, Luther, by example as well as by precept, founded the Protestant parsonage and pioneered the modern Christian home. To the Christian believer, who finds sanctity not in artificial priestcraft but in doing God's will within

---

[12] WA XII, 490.

the natural frameworks in which God places men, to be ashamed of marriage is to be ashamed of being a man and to try to "improve upon the work of God." The Christian has learned already from the fourth commandment, in which "God has done marriage the honor of putting it . . . immediately after the honor due Him," that "in God's sight there is no higher office, estate, condition, and work (next to the Gospel which concerns God himself) than the estate of marriage."[13] On the other hand, broken marriage ties are traced "to the fact that men do not regard marriage according to God's Word as His work and ordinance, do not pay regard to His will," but "regard it as nothing else than a mere human, secular affair, with which God has nothing to do."[14] Luther placed particular emphasis upon the home as a place for training in Christian character and exercise of Christian virtues. It was, to his mind, a thousand times better suited to this purpose than were the monasteries. The importance which he ascribed to religious education in the home is reflected by the fact that his Small Catechism was written with this end in view. No Christians exercise a higher priestly function than Christian parents who teach their children the Word of God.

The state, as well as the Church and the home, is for Luther a divinely appointed order. It is a fellowship of

---

[13] *Works* (Holman ed.), III, 423.

[14] *Commentary on the Sermon on the Mount,* tr. C. A. Hay (Philadelphia: United Lutheran Publication House, 1892), p. 169.

force, doing the work of God's left hand, while the
Church is a fellowship of love, doing the work of God's
right hand. This view is correlated with Luther's basic
conception of love as "opus Dei proprium," and of
wrath and judgment as "opus Dei alienum." The state
is "the servant of God's wrath" and rulers are "Christ's
hangmen." Unlike many subsequent German thinkers,
Luther did not idealize the state nor glorify power for
its own sake. "We are not obligated," he says, "to be
obedient to secular authority for its own sake . . . but
for the sake of God whose children we are."[15] It is true
that Luther owed much to those German princes who
at great risk to themselves supported the Reformation.
But those who accuse Luther of instilling in the German people an attitude of servility toward a totalitarian
state forget that these comparatively petty Protestant
princes, far from representing totalitarian government,
were engaged in the very effort to resist imperial totali-
tarianism. Nor must Luther's dependence upon them
be exaggerated. To the Reformer, the state is the realm
of sin and can do nothing positive toward the advance-
ment of God's Kingdom. But God can use it, as He does
the devil himself, for His ultimate good purposes. The
function of the state is to furnish protection, to punish
evildoers, to use force in keeping violence and disorder
in check. In carrying out this function the state main-
tains conditions under which the Gospel can do the
constructive work of the Kingdom.   The state itself

---
[15] WA XII, 328.

cannot be ruled by the Gospel. Luther's sober realism is in sharp contrast with the sentimental utopianism which marks much of later Protestant social thought: ". . . first take heed and fill the world with real Christians before ruling it in a Christian and evangelical manner. This you will never accomplish; for the world and the masses are and always will be unchristian, although they are all baptized and are nominally Christian. Christians, however, are few and far between. . . . Therefore it is out of the question that there should be a common Christian government over the whole world, nay, even over one land or company of people, since the wicked always outnumber the good. Hence a man who would venture to govern an entire country or the world with the Gospel would be like a shepherd who should place in one fold wolves, lions, eagles, and sheep together and let them freely mingle with one another and say, Help yourselves; the fold is open, there is plenty of food; have no fear of dogs and clubs. The sheep, forsooth, would keep the peace and would allow themselves to be fed and governed in peace, but they would not live long. . . ."[16] To expect the state to do good and promote love, in the Christian sense, is sheer hypocrisy. "The worldly kingdom, which is nothing but the servant of divine wrath over evil and a true forerunner of hell and eternal death, shall not be kind, but severe, serious, and angry."[17] But unless the state

---

[16] WA XI, 251.

[17] WA XVIII, 389.

directly opposes the Gospel and violates Christian conscience, "we should fear all earthly law and order as
God's will and law."[18] For even harsh and unjust rule
is preferable to anarchy.

Under these conditions the channel through which
Christian influence most effectively flows into the political order is the universal priesthood of believers. When
the secular authorities are Christians, they can be de-
pended upon to do everything within their power to
give the Word of God free course. In this spirit Luther
enlisted the aid of the German princes in bringing
about the Reformation, when his appeals to church
authorities went unheeded. In the same spirit he asked
the secular authorities to establish and promote Christian schools. A Christian ruler must remember his
higher calling as spiritual priest and king. The more
power or influence a Christian wields, the greater will
be his opportunity and his responsibility for Christian
service. Such service is sorely needed in high places,
for, according to Luther, "from the beginning of the
world a wise prince has been a rare bird, and a pious
prince still more rare. They are usually the greatest
fools or the worst rascals on earth."[19] Conditions will
not improve until our Lord God makes more Christians,
among rulers as well as among subjects, Christians who
will act as Christians in whatever position God places
them.

[18] WA XXVI, 211.
[19] WA XI, 267.

Thus the priesthood of believers extends, finally, beyond the political realm into the economic order and into every vocation. No one has excelled Luther in condemning laziness and parasitism, whether secular or churchly, and in praising the dignity of every form of honest work. Every useful occupation, no matter how lowly in the eyes of the world, is a God-given calling in which a Christian man is offered a unique opportunity to serve God and fellow-man. Thus, "if he is a Christian tailor, he says, 'My object in making this coat is to do what God has bidden me to do and to be of service, so that by this means I can help and serve my neighbor.'"[20] From the abolition of the caste system in the Church and the restoration of laymen to their original status in the Christian fellowship follows the revolutionary discovery that there are no special sacred zones in life but that everyday toil can become worship. This discovery contains a wealth of new dynamic insights. It deals a death blow to the Greek and medieval conception which places the contemplative life above the active. It gives incentive and freedom of research to the natural and practical sciences, and opens the door to technical development. It introduces Christian love as the dominant motive in every occupation and judges every enterprise from that point of view. It transforms the negatives of religion into positives, enabling Luther, for example, to interpret "Thou shalt not steal" as implying: work and earn your own living so that you may

---

[20] WA XI, 382.

have something to give to the needy; to be idle is to rob your needy neighbor.[21] It puts an end to compartmentalization and makes the service motive, as over against the profit motive, a Christian responsibility in every situation. It acknowledges that the world is evil, but instead of counseling escape or retreat, it summons every Christian to be an outlet for the leavening influence of the Kingdom. It provides the social program of the Church with its most effective method, not the construction of utopias or futile frontal attacks upon established systems, but the same personal witnessing by word and act to the life-changing power of the Gospel, which enabled the primitive church to win its victories. To use one of Luther's most telling metaphors, it calls every Christian to be the disguise under which God can enter even where He is not openly welcome.

II. UNIVERSAL SPIRITUAL PRIESTHOOD
IN THE LIGHT OF TODAY

When Charles P. Taft, a layman, recently became president of the Federal Council of the Churches of Christ in America, he said, "The world cries for the effective and universal Christian ministry of all believers." No profound meditation on the present world-situation is required to establish the truth of this statement. We are beset with many uncertainties, but of one thing we can be absolutely certain: we are facing a world of great and distressing needs. One cannot

---

[21.] EA IX, 319.

reduce men to be cogs in a ruthless and soulless machine of destruction without reaping the consequences. As Dr. Harry E. Fosdick once expressed it, "You cannot suck the egg of personality's value and then hatch a high religion out of it." What you do hatch is fears, hatreds, anxieties, a loss of the sense of the worth-while-ness of living. When life has been made cheap and sordid and hard, the inevitable letdown comes sooner or later in vicious life-adjustments such as irresponsibility, drunkenness, and crime. If ever the Church had a ministry to broken hearts and twisted and warped minds, it needs to apply it now. The needs of individuals are matched by those of the home and of the community. The demoralizing and hardening influences of the day have attacked the Church's most important ally, the home, with unprecedented ferocity. Divorce and disloyalty are rampant. Children, lacking Christian atmosphere and guidance in the home, are straying into the wild paths of delinquency. There is scarcely a community which does not face such enormous problems as regards home conditions, economic readjustment, child welfare, youth guidance, decency and morality, that all agencies for good must be mobilized to meet them. Nor can anyone escape direct contact with the broader nationwide problems, such as the tensions between capital and labor, so vividly brought home by recent strikes. Finally, the needs of the whole community of nations have suddenly come very near. Isolationism has become impossible, for we know now that the world has shrunk to such small proportions that whatever concerns people in any corner of it is also our concern. And we now face the problem of being neighbors with organized and powerful anti-Christian forces.

We face something worse than a pagan world, one which does not know Christ. Ours is a generation involved in the deeper tragedy of having perverted to destructive ends the spiritual energies released by Christ. To call an apostate Christian culture barbaric is to slander the barbarians.

Confronted with such a world the Church cannot carry out its mission without recovering universal spiritual priesthood in all its original power. What has happened to this vital insight even among those who are heirs of the Reformation has been dramatically portrayed by Dr. Robert E. Speer: "The minister is to be simply colonel of the regiment. The real fighting is to be done by the men in the ranks who carry the guns. No ideal could be more non-Christian or more irrational than that the religious colonel is engaged to do the fighting for his men, while they sit at ease. And yet, perhaps, there is one idea current which is more absurd still, that is, that there is to be no fighting at all, but that the colonel is paid to spend his time solacing his regiment, or giving it gentle educative instruction, not destined even to result in any downright, manly effort on the part of the whole regiment to do anything against the enemy."[22]

[22.] Quoted from John R. Mott, *op. cit.*, p. 42.

In attempting to restate the constructive meaning of the priesthood of all believers for the present day, let me lay down three propositions: (1) To be a Christian is to be a member of a fellowship. (2) To be a member of the fellowship is to be consecrated to bear witness. (3) To bear witness is to serve Christ within the divinely appointed frameworks of life.

1. *Membership in the Christian fellowship.* In the first of these propositions, to be a Christian is to be a member of a fellowship, we seek to recapture the original emphasis in the apostolic concept of the royal priesthood upon membership in the messianic nation. No insight in twentieth-century Christian thinking is more significant than the rediscovery of the Church. We have awakened to the fact that Christianity is not a set of opinions that we think about but a fellowship in which we share. It is a dynamic nucleus for the integration of human life. It binds people together. It unites the followers of Christ into a household of faith for worship and for work together. To say that a Christian is an individual answerable only to God is simply untrue. God has set him to live out his life, not in isolated privacy, but within divinely appointed frameworks of living. He is never a mere private individual. He cannot escape being a member. Just as he is a member of a home, of a community, and of a nation, so in the matter of religion he is a member of the Church.

Such membership is not an arbitrary thing which I can take or leave as my whim happens to be. It is a part of God's plan for my life. He meant me to be a church member just as He meant me to be a son or daughter in a home and a citizen in a state. The Church is not of man's making. People did not come together and organize the Church as they would organize a luncheon club or a literary society. The Church is the colony of heaven on earth, the continuation and fruition in history of the life which Christ implanted in it. "I am the vine," says Christ, "you are the branches." One does not first have branches and by putting them together form the vine. "You are the body of Christ," says Paul. One does not first have eyes, ears, hands, feet, and other separate members and then unite them to form the body. The Church exists before any of its individual members. Its existence is rooted in God's eternal purpose. When He elected to redeem me He elected me into a fellowship of the redeemed. Vital Christian experience, therefore, cannot help being churchly experience. It is generated by the Holy Spirit through the Word and the sacraments which are not the property of any individual but the means of grace given to the Church. Hence no individual is "the body of Christ." The Church is the body of Christ, and the individual has a living organic relation to Christ only as he is a member of the organism. Neither is any individual "the bride of Christ." It is only as a member of the fellowship that he has the right to appropriate for himself the benefits of this relation of love. It is of the Church that we sing:

"From heaven He came and sought her
   To be His holy bride;
With His own blood He bought her
   And for her life He died."

My choice, then, as a Christian is not between being a church member and not being one. I *am* one by the very nature of the case. The choice is only whether I am a good member or a bad one, a living member or a dead one. If God is my Father, then I must take my place in the family of God's children. Otherwise I am a vagabond. The Church is my spiritual home, the beloved community in which the pattern of human brotherhood based on divine fatherhood is carried out. In it burdens are lifted, the fallen set on their feet, the sorrowful comforted, the weary made strong. For it is a royal priesthood in which each is consecrated to serve the other as "Christs one to another." But it is also a *universal* priesthood. What it does to me in unifying my life and uniting it with that of others, in the Spirit of Christ, it can do to all men. Just as sin divides mankind and sets brother against brother, so the forgiveness of sins in Christ unites mankind and creates that Society of the Spirit, that fellowship of forgiveness, which is the Church. When men in their sinful pride and stupidity set up barriers of nation, class, and race, the only hope for universal brotherhood lies in the universal spiritual priesthood.

2. *Bearing witness.* Our second proposition is: to be a member of the fellowship is to bear witness. A Chris-

tian is not a private person from the point of view of the world outside any more than from the point of view of the fellowship within. He is a marked man. He is a witness, an epistle of Christ, the salt of the earth. The treasure of the fellowship is given to him to do business with; unless he returns it with interest it is taken away from him. The Church provides not only a home for the whole family of God's children but also a workshop. The blessing of Christ's presence is inseparably connected with obedience to the mission He has given to go forth and evangelize in every human contact. The deepest meaning of the incarnation lies here: the divine makes its strongest impact upon us, God becomes most real to us, when He assumes the human touch, is lived out, and touches us. Just so Christian men and women are the original means of grace, the agencies by which God works. Universal priesthood means that every Christian is a God-appointed channel through whom the grace and power of Christ flow into the common life of humanity to hallow it.

Most church members are poor witnesses because the upper story of their life, which ought to be the domain of spiritual growth, is only an attic housing old relics and curiosities. Consequently they can tell only what others are supposed to have seen and heard but which they themselves have never experienced. When they recite the sublime creeds or sing the lofty hymns of the Church, it is as if they had been dropped to these mountain heights from an airplane by parachute. "Jesus, my

Lord, my God, my All," I may sing. But is He that to me? What is there in my life that requires Christ to explain it? Our use of religious phrases is often empty repetition without any ring of sincerity. There is hardly anything more tragic than to find a lifelong "Christian" who in the hour of need has no sound spiritual resources. He has words and language but nothing back of them. There is truth in the saying, "No one has more religion than he can command in an emergency." It is not sincere religion lightly to appropriate as one's own spiritual values for which saints have struggled a lifetime. Such spirituality is as sterile as it is counterfeit. Moody was doubtless right in insisting that no man can bring another nearer Christ than he is himself. Before exhorting nominal Christians to bear witness for Christ we do well to heed Kierkegaard's plea for a little common honesty in these high matters.

Some influence we exert, some witness we bear, in any case, knowingly or unknowingly. Radium was discovered because it made itself felt by its glow, by throwing off particles of itself. Just so, whether we are aware of it or not, we throw vibrations from ourselves to elevate or to degrade the lives of others. Even when it is not engaged in direct religious activity, Christian personality, sensitized to the living Christ, is radiant with spiritual reality and transmissive of divine presence. But such a person cannot witness only silently and unconsciously. "Out of the fullness of the heart the mouth speaketh." Witnessing becomes a conscious obligation. It is a duty so personal that no Christian can perform it for another. As Dr. Franklin C. Fry has expressed it, "Just as no one can love my wife and my children for me, so no one can witness to my Saviour for me." From the beginning Christianity has been a contact game. Andrew meets Christ, Andrew brings to Him his brother Peter, and Peter leads thousands to Christ. We see the big results and give credit to the people directly responsible for them. Often the people back of the big people with the big influence go unnoticed. We hear about a powerful Christian movement in postwar Japan, with tens of thousands of converts, and we reaffirm our estimate of its leader Kagawa as being one of the greatest of living Christians. But few have heard even the name of H. W. Myers, the unsung Christian who led Kagawa to Christ.

3. *Serving within the frameworks.* Our third proposition is: to be a witness is to serve Christ within the divinely created frameworks of life. This means a restoration of Luther's vigorous emphasis on the *calling* and on the *orders of creation.* Here lies one of the most fruitful fields of theological research in our time. A list of European theologians who have written on the "orders" includes such names as Gogarten, Hirsch, Althaus, and Kuenneth in Germany, Brunner in Switzerland, Runestam in Sweden, and Jalkanen in Finland. It has been said that this doctrine became as popular in Germany during the thirties as the Trinity in the days of Athanasius and justification by faith during the

Reformation. It was a featured dogma in the Ecumenical Conference at Oxford in 1937. The fact that we in America have heard so little about it may be due to a large extent to its misuse by some German scholars to support the Nazi deification of "blood and soil." While theologians are by no means agreed either as to the concept itself or its scope, we may, with Althaus and Brunner, designate as orders of creation the forms of human corporate life which are the indispensable presuppositions of the historical existence of men, binding them to each other in definite ways and causing them to serve one another. In opposition to irresponsible individualism in every sphere, this concept stands for the truth that the basic forms of human society are part of the creative work of God, that human life is life in community, and that no one is a mere private person but a member having a God-given place and calling in every important area of the common life. Not only in the Church but also in the home, the state, and in the economic and cultural orders, we have divinely given conditions of life and consequently also divinely appointed tasks. It is God who has made us responsible to each other, to be at once givers and receivers. His will meets us in actual circumstances, in the concrete situations of our life with each other. Both the individual by himself and society by itself are abstractions, for to be a human individual is to have responsible existence in society. To base life on either alone, to use

Brunner's metaphor, is like hanging a suspension bridge from a single tower.

We thus obtain a Christian philosophy of society, which is at once realistic and profound. Life in love is not an idle dream or a pious sentimentality. It is the ground plan of all creation. It is the will of the Creator that we must learn to live together if we are to live at all, although stupid infidelity requires costly trial-and-error methods to ascertain this fact. Natural morality can only balance the claims of individuals and of groups; it can create no genuine fellowship. It was through Christ, the Logos, that all the orders of life were made, and it is only in Him that they become meaningful and workable. On the other hand, we must acknowledge that ours is a fallen creation and that all its orders are subject to sin and death. Concerning our social, as well as intellectual, frameworks, we must say,

> "Our little systems have their day,
>   They have their day and cease to be.
>   They are but broken lights of Thee,
>   And Thou, O Lord, art more than they."

Our systems have no true autonomy or permanence. God remains sovereign and judge over them, and because of their sinfulness will eventually destroy them. But within a world marked for doom a new order, that of redemption, is already at work, and its hope is a new heaven and a new earth. It is through Christ's resurrection, as Kuenneth in his *Theologie der Auferstehung* has pointed out, that the power of the new creation has burst forth into the present world to take away the curse of sin and the wrath of judgment and to carry out the purpose of God, who predestined His creation to Christlikeness. Christians who have "risen with Christ into a newness of life" are the channels through which this power is released into the world. The life of the Christian in society is a constant tension between the inner structure of the personal life and its outer framework, the duty to transform and the need to conform. A Christian statesman or businessman has to abide by the laws and methods of politics and economics, if he is to do anything at all, although they fall far short of Christian ideals. But he is also under obligation to do all in his power to criticize and change these procedures in the light of the higher standards he acknowledges. Most of his actual choices will be not between absolute right and absolute wrong but between greater and lesser evils, for no sinless alternative will be present. In such a conflict of loyalties a Christian can nevertheless act with confidence and a clear conscience when he is aware of a divine calling within the sinful environment. As Kierkegaard insisted, when a man chooses to be a Christian he chooses to suffer. But he will carry out the duties of his calling and live by the grace of forgiveness.

This Christian social philosophy applies to each of the orders. As regards the home and marriage, it means that the existence of the family is not grounded, as secular theories have held, upon a natural desire for self-gratification but upon the will of the Creator. "Male and female created He them." We may stress with Otto Piper that union between man and woman brings about such an essential unity between complementary beings that by the very nature of the case it cannot be broken, and that in the exercise of this unity there is such a sacred mutual self-disclosure that it cannot be communicated to, or shared with, others, without violating it. Or we may point with Emil Brunner to the eternal and indestructible trinity of father-mother-child. Every father is irrevocably with this one woman, and every mother with this one man, the father and mother of this child, and every human being is irrevocably the child of one man and one woman. A personal relationship is thus created which nothing can sever because it is God's own doing. When the marriage bond is thus seen to consist not in individual passion or social expediency but in God's will, then its proper virtue will be seen to be not the negative one of abstinence but positive purity of heart, responsible love and loyalty.

In the Christian perspective the state, too, is a divinely appointed order. It exists for the purpose of preserving order, establishing justice, and creating community, thus providing the conditions under which spiritual ideals may be realized. But here, as perhaps nowhere else, the Christian faces a conflict between his highest loyalties and the imponderable realities of a sinful world. A case in point is the question of bearing arms when the existence of the state is endangered. To deny the state the right to use force for self-protection is to deny the state the right to exist. But the individual Christian is trapped in a dilemma: to fight involves the sin of taking life; not to fight involves civic disobedience and ingratitude, and may mean support of injustice. The decision must be left in each case to Christian conscience while methods for abolishing the tragic dilemma are sought. At all events, whether he is a plain citizen or an office-holder, a Christian cannot shirk his obligations in the political order, for to him they are God-given obligations. While the negative duty of criticism must be exercised so long as the state is vitiated by sinful corruption, we may well ask: is there not a greater need in our chaotic day to stress with Luther the constructive virtue of law-abiding obedience to constituted authority? Even an imperfect rule, as the Reformer saw, is better than an anarchy of conflicting interests.

It is particularly in the economic order, in the realm of daily work, that the Christian has his calling to live out his Christianity. The Church as an institution has specific limitations here which can be overcome by the Church as universal spiritual priesthood. Using an example from the late Archbishop Temple, "If a bridge is to be built, the Church may remind the engineer that it is his obligation to build a really safe bridge but is not entitled to tell him whether, in fact, his design meets this requirement."[23]   The institutional Church cannot be an expert in engineering or in any other field of daily work. But the Church can and must send forth not only engineers but also physicians, lawyers, teachers, mechanics, and farmers, men in every occupation who combine Christian ideals with their technical knowledge and ability, and therefore translate these ideals into concrete reality. In this way the Church can work far more effectively than by drawing up well-meant but amateurish and impractical economic and political programs.

The Lutheran type of Christianity has often been charged with social defeatism and inertia because it has refused to believe that the efforts of sinful men can bring in the Kingdom of God. If human efforts cannot bring in the Kingdom, the inference is: why do anything at all? According to George W. Forell, when this question was put to a European professor of theology, he gave the following answer: "A surgeon who is operating on a patient stricken with appendicitis does not believe that because he may be successful in this operation the patient will never die. In this sense the surgeon does not believe that the operation has ultimate significance. Yet he will try everything in his power to prolong his patient's life to the best of his ability. He is a doctor. To preserve human life is his calling. He must be faithful to his calling. The fact that his efforts will

---

[23.] W. Temple, *Christianity and the Social Order* (New York: Penguin Books, 1942), chap. 2.

be ultimately frustrated, since nobody can escape death, does not enter into his considerations."[24] It is not necessary to harbor illusions about the facts of sin and death, as regards either cultures or individual persons, in order to do constructive work for the betterment of society. A Rousseau with his faith in the goodness of man and his lofty theories of social reform sends his own children to an asylum for foundlings, while a Francke, deeply disturbed by his sins which to other people are as inconspicuous as Rousseau's are obvious, builds an orphanage. The men and women who in the grind of everyday life seek to obey God and to maintain a good conscience before Him by carrying out the responsibilities of their calling in faith and in love are the true "salt of the earth." Their names may not appear in newspaper headlines, to say nothing of history textbooks, and yet like the hidden stream of oil which Bunyan's Pilgrim saw keeping the flame burning in the midst of the winds, they pour forth a silent but sustaining and transforming influence for the good. Often they afford remarkable illustrations for our Lord's saying, "He that loses his life will find it." Apparently lost in complete obscurity, their faith may find a rich and strong expression in lives they have affected. There are, for example, unmistakable Christian elements in Karl Marx's revolutionary championing of the economically disinherited, elements which have sometimes been

---

[24.] "The Christian Basis for Social Action," *Christian Opinion*, II (January, 1945), No. 2.

traced to the Hebrew prophets. What is not generally known is that Marx's father was a converted Jew, a Lutheran Christian, and that something of the spirit of Him who came to preach good tidings to the poor entered into Marx's thought through this channel. It may not be amiss to regard the elder Marx as symbolic in this respect of the Church of the Gospel and the younger Marx as representative of the economic and political forces as such. It is the business of the secular power directly to attack natural evils, such as poverty and unemployment and other unwholesome and unjust social conditions. And it is the business of the Church to sensitize the consciences of men to the existence of these conditions, to give a vision of the goals to be sought, and to create the will to seek them. The Church deals primarily and directly, however, not with any impersonal order or set of conditions, but with individual conscience. Hence its own specific operations are directed against personal moral evil rather than against impersonal or natural evil. A political and economic philosophy, whether Marxian or any other, proceeds on the principle of *causality* to analyze, to manipulate, or to change *conditions*. The Church proceeds on the principle of *responsibility* to diagnose and to change *men*. The Church finds the deepest source of man's trouble not in his political maladjustment or economic misery but in his defiance of God. And, instead of allowing the individual to shift the blame from himself to external circumstances, it sharpens his personal accountability to God. But it not only gives this deeper diagnosis of man's predicament but also makes available to him the healing power of divine forgiveness and the sustaining strength of the Christian fellowship, empowering him to minister constructively to the same basic need of other men, the need of personal salvation.

The social philosophy of the Gospel is thus vastly different from the so-called Social Gospel. When Shailer Mathews, a typical exponent of the latter, defined the Kingdom of God as "an ideal, though progressively approximated, social order in which the relation of men to God is that of sons, and therefore to each other, that of brothers,"[25] and called on all Christians to help build such an order, he was presenting a concept and a program of which Christ said nothing. Christ spoke of no developmental bridge from our social order to God's Kingdom. He did not ask us to build God a Kingdom but to confess "Thine *is* the Kingdom," to acknowledge that the Kingdom "comes" to us on its own power, to realize that in Him it had already come, to receive it and to be committed to it in faith, to bear witness to it in word and deed, and confidently to leave its future to God himself. The superficiality of the social and moral activism which has masqueraded as "building the Kingdom of God" has been aptly characterized by George Tyrrell as "going about doing good, particularly the kind of doing good which involves a great deal of

---

[25.] *The Social Teaching of Jesus* (New York: Macmillan, 1897), p. 54.

going about." The Gospel knows nothing about a Christian economic or political system. It builds men who are radiant centers of Christian influence in any system and who are not disheartened by the failure of any system. Christians are called to be Christians wherever they are, including the political and economic spheres, and to identify themselves in any given situation with the cause which Christian conscience judges to be nearest Christian ideals. But it is sinful stupidity and arrogance to consider any system of man's making, ecclesiastical or secular, as God's Kingdom.

Forsaking the false optimism of the age of evolutionism, we must acknowledge the tragic character of human history implied in Christ's description of the world as a field in which wheat and tares grow together until the day of judgment. In the final analysis, we must apply to society as a whole, even with the Gospel at work within it, the same term which Luther applied to the individual believer: "simul iustus et peccator." We must expect the tension between the Kingdom of God and the Kingdom of Evil to mount, not to slacken, in intensity. The evildoer will "still do evil . . . and the righteous still do right" (Rev. 22:11), in increasing measure and with greater maturity and effectiveness, until the last act of the drama of history, when God himself will resolve the tension with the ultimate triumph of His Kingdom on the day of Christ. Until that day the fellowship of God's people must live in the same world side by side with more and more powerful and diabolical forces of evil. But the Christian fellow-ship, true to its Lord and drawing upon His resources, has always known how to act in such circumstances. As in the first century, wherever the life of a Christian touches another life, there the leaven of the Kingdom is at work through the priesthood of all believers. Not only where a congregation gathers for worship, but where a Christian father gathers his household to hear the Word of God, or where a Christian workingman tells his fellow-laborer what has taken place in his life because of what Christ has done, there is the Church of Christ. And against that Church the gates of hell will not prevail.

CHAPTER V

THE THEOLOGY OF THE GOSPEL IN ACTION

WE HAVE STUDIED the key principles of the evangelical faith: justifying grace which establishes the right relation between man and God, the living Word which is the instrument of that grace, and the universal priesthood which the Word creates and consecrates. We have seen the relevance of that faith to the needs of the present day and gained an insight into why its resurgence has brought new depth and vitality to contemporary theological thinking. The question still remains: how can this theology be translated into a program of action in order that it may also revitalize the Church and make its impact as a living force on contemporary life? A mere restatement of ancient dogmas cannot take the place of a rediscovery of the religious life which they express. Even a correct theological formula is no more effective in satisfying man's need of God than the correct chemical formula for water in quenching his thirst. Saying the right things about God, insists Luther, contributes as little to salvation as dressing a scoundrel in the garb of a monk makes him a man of God. What constructive methods, then, toward the generation of true and vital faith grow out of the ground of basic evangelical theology?

In an important but hitherto little known writing published in 1528, Luther himself goes far toward answering this question. It is entitled *Instructions to Ministers to be Given by the Visitors of Churches.*[1] The Reformer is distressed by the observation that there are pastors who set forth the faith by which men become righteous and yet "they do not show clearly enough how one can come to this faith." Their failure is traced to forgetting Christ's own instruction: "repentance and remission of sins should be preached in his name" (Luke 24:47). Preachers err when they think they can preach the Gospel of the forgiveness of sins while saying little or nothing about repentance. "And yet the forgiveness of sins cannot even be understood without repentance." When forgiveness is preached without repentance people are lulled into a false security which is more dangerous than all the errors of Rome. Ministers are therefore to be instructed that they are under obligation to preach the whole Gospel and not one part of it without the other. "They should diligently and often admonish people to repentance, to have contrition and anguish over their sins and to be frightened on account of God's judgment." Nor should they forget that Christ reproved the Pharisees for their hypocrisy more severely than for ordinary sins. "Therefore the preachers should rebuke the people for gross sins, but

---

[1] WA XXVI, 202 ff.

they should still more earnestly admonish to repentance where there is false holiness." When such admonition has led to penitence and anguish for sins, it is then necessary to present clearly the justifying faith which "makes righteous and destroys sin." The terrified and penitent conscience must be given that peace, consolation, and joy which flow from the forgiveness of sins. But "people must be diligently advised that this faith cannot come about without serious and true repentance and terror of conscience before God." Without such an emphasis people will "fall into self-deception and suppose that they have faith although they are far from it." Where there is no true repentance there can be no true comfort or joy, and faith is only a "painted faith."

So important is this matter to Luther that he returns again and again to the same basic emphasis: where there is no genuine repentance there is no genuine faith. He sums up the relation between contrition and faith in a meaty formula: "Contrition without faith is despair; and faith without contrition is arrogance and carnal security." The natural tendency in human nature is "to fabricate a faith." A man may assent to the true proposition that "his whole nature is evil" and yet have no inkling of that true knowledge of sin which means "that one is burdened under contrition and grief on account of sin, being in his heart terrified because of God's wrath and judgment." David knew well enough that he had sinned, but he knew no contrition until Nathan had rebuked him. Unless a preacher today just as fearlessly rebukes people's sins, God will hold him responsible for their souls. He must therefore deal straightforwardly with "drunkenness, lewdness, envy, hatred, greed, lying" and other specific sins, and he should show that "God's wrath is upon the false worshipers of God or hypocrites, who blaspheme God's name by their holy appearance." Nor can he escape his responsibility by arguing that God himself must work repentance and faith in men's hearts. "It is true that God works true repentance, but He effects it through the Word and preaching. In the same manner people are to be encouraged to faith, and yet God works faith through preaching."

If these "instructions to ministers" were timely a decade after the beginning of the Reformation, they are even more so now that four centuries lie between us and the vital faith of the Reformation. Luther's fear that the rediscovered Gospel had as little chance of escaping corruption as did the original Gospel appears to have been well founded. The "painted faith" against which Luther warned, the substitution of external and impersonal representations for a direct personal contact with God himself, exists in numerous forms even among those professing to be Luther's heirs.

Often the object of such painted faith is the organized Church itself. An old and respectable religious institution easily changes from an instrumentality into an end in itself. Our Lord's fight for the Kingdom of God was against a powerful churchliness, and His bitterest enemies were High Priests. Luther's devotion to the Gospel led to an inevitable break with an ecclesiastical institution which demanded for its own ordinances the honor and obedience due to God. There is a depth of truth in the scriptural doctrine that the devil himself was once an angel led astray by inordinate self-esteem. Luther was thoroughly consistent with this truth in discovering the Antichrist not outside the Church but within it, in its highest seat of power, the papacy. But we, the followers of Luther, do well to engage at this point in some searching self-criticism. For there is more than just a subtle hint of Satanic pride in our boast: ours is the church which has the Gospel in its pure and unadulterated form. Judgment must begin in the house of God. We must confess that we have sinned in presenting our formulations of divine truth as though they were the divine truth itself, final and unalterable and worthy of men's highest loyalty. The danger of betraying the evangelical spirit is present whenever emphasis shifts from the activity of God in men's hearts to the works of men's hands. The latter may take the form of erecting magnificent buildings, of perfecting efficient institutional machinery, of enlisting large groups of people. All this activity performs a useful function when its purely secondary and instrumental character is borne in mind. The primary business of the Church is being transacted not when hundreds of delegates are in session to elect committees and set up budgets, but when a pastor or a layman is using the Word to relieve a sin-distressed conscience. Leslie Weatherhead has estimated that ninety per cent of churchgoing people have no vital experience of Christ and hence also no sense of spiritual power. If this be the case, is it not largely because we have allowed people to fall into the error of supposing that if they believe what the Church believes and do their best to carry out the obligations of external church membership, they are Christians and have no need of personal repentance and faith? Our churches are becoming so respectable that the probing of individual consciences with a view to bringing about repentance, such as Luther counsels, is likely to be regarded as impertinence and bad taste.

A similar confusion of ends and means may take place as regards the Church's means of grace, with the result that the Word and the Sacraments become the objects of painted faith. It has already been pointed out that to accept the Bible as true, or even infallible, is an inadequate substitute for the living Word. If Luther is right in his insistence that there is no true faith where there is no contrition, we may have to reappraise our entire system of religious education, no matter how Bible-centered it may be. Said one Lutheran pastor to a group of others: "Ask any of your confirmands to answer the question, 'Are you a sinner?' and he will promptly answer 'Yes,' but in the answer there will be no humility or penitence because he is a sinner but rather pride because he has given the right answer." Columba brought about such penitence among the

Franks that they signed themselves "sinners." But in the course of time the term "sinner" came to be to the Franks a badge of honor and boasting. Unless the instruction given in our church schools and catechetical classes reaches beyond mere knowledge to the conscience and leads to genuine personal commitment to Christ, then our educational system is turning out at best respectable church members, not regenerated Christians. To confirm a child at twelve or thirteen, as is generally done, and not to expect any further specific religious decision after that is neither theologically nor psychologically sound. Even if the pastor should try his best to make clear to the confirmand the importance of confirmation as a personal decision to be a Christian, repentance and faith at that early age can have only superficial meaning. They would mean much more in the sixteenth or seventeenth year when the conflict between spirit and flesh has become a reality and the sense of personal responsibility has matured. If confirmation is to be the principal method for entrance into responsible membership in the church, then confirmation at twelve is admirably suited to the Roman Catholic ideal of a membership early and thoroughly indoctrinated in the beliefs and behavior patterns of the organization and resolved to render docile loyalty to it. But in the Church of the Gospel, where the objective is nothing less than the direct faith-relationship of the individual with Christ himself and personal assurance of His grace, the evangelistic note must be the dominant one in every form of preparation for church membership.

The theology of the Gospel demands that the Sacraments, too, be made to serve a living, not a painted, faith. In accordance with apostolic faith and practice, baptism must be regarded as the basis for Christian life and fellowship. It is through baptism, declares Paul, that we die with Christ and rise with Him into a newness of life. It is by that means that the justifying and renewing grace of God comes to be applied to individ= ual persons. Evangelical theology has always taken seriously our Lord's words, "make disciples . . . baptizing them," and has seen the inseparable connection between baptism and regeneration: "Except a man be born of water and of the Spirit, he cannot enter into the kingdom of God" (John 3:5) and "According to his mercy he saved us, through the washing of regeneration and renewing of the Holy Ghost" (Titus 3:5).   In further agreement with apostolic faith and practice, classical Protestant theology recognizes the baptism of *infants* as a uniquely significant portrayal of the spirit of the Gospel. Here, if anywhere, we have a demonstration of "prevenient grace," of the divine love which takes the initiative and makes salvation possible for the helpless. The Good Shepherd does not wait until the little ones are big enough and strong enough and wise enough to find their way into the fold. As beautifully portrayed in the parable of the lost sheep, while they are as utterly helpless as a stray lamb caught in the brambles and prey to any wolf that may happen along, He comes to them, seeks them out, rescues them, carries them home. If such divine activity did not precede our own, we could never be quite sure of reaching the point when we qualify for admission into God's Kingdom. It was because he saw so deeply into the heart of the Gospel that Luther derived so much comfort from the thought that in his infancy he had been taken into God's covenant of grace. Baptism was to him essentially "the sacrament of little ones" who had nothing of their own to offer and therefore had to receive everything by grace alone. True to this spirit, great leaders in movements of spiritual awakening in the Lutheran countries, as for example Grundtvig of Denmark, have regarded true revival as a return to baptismal grace. Over against those who have ridiculed "water baptism" and resorted to their own methods of whipping up spirituality, the heirs of the evangelical legacy have remembered Luther's warning: "Whatever is boasted of the spirit outside the word and the sacraments is of the devil."[2]

Such recognition of baptism as the divinely laid foundation of the Christian life and means of grace does not permit us, however, to regard every baptized person as a true child of God. While God's covenant with us in baptism remains eternal and unbroken on His side, we may sever our relation to it through disobedience and unbelief. In Luther's pictorial language, while baptismal grace is a ship carrying us safely to heaven, we may

---

[2] *Smalcald Articles,* VIII.

fall overboard. So widespread and so persistent appeared to the Reformer this falling away from Christ on the part of "Christians" that he was led to say, "The world and the masses are . . . unchristian even though they are all baptized" and to hold that "true Christians are few and far between." Baptismal water, he insisted, has no more inherent spiritual efficacy than the water which the cow drinks or which the housemaid uses in cooking. It is the Word which makes it "a gracious water of life and washing of regeneration" and that Word requires the vital personal response of repentance and faith. Whether the individual's religious experience represents a gradual deepening of the faith of childhood or a return to it after an acknowledged break, Luther's principle still holds: where there is no contrition there is no true faith. The "Lutheran" who supposes that the doors of heaven will be opened to him when he simply produces his baptismal certificate needs to be reminded of Luther's definition of the significance of baptism: "It signifies that the old Adam in us should, by daily sorrow and repentance, be drowned and die, with all sins and evil lusts; and again a new man daily come forth and arise, who shall live before God in righteousness and purity forever."

In the sacrament of the altar the evangelical faith receives its highest conceivable expression. Here the sinner and his Saviour come face to face to consummate that "blessed exchange" signified by justification, the exchange of the sinner's sin for Christ's righteousness.

Here God in His grace bestows upon each individual believer His most precious gift, the forgiveness of sins, and "where there is forgiveness of sins, there is also life and salvation." "The chief thing in this sacrament," as Luther points out, is contained in the words "given and shed for you for the remission of sins," and this is the chief thing in the entire Gospel. Since "the words 'for you' require truly believing hearts," we can have no better standard for membership in the fellowship of Christ's redeemed people than participation in the Communion in sincere repentance and faith. It is altogether proper, therefore, for the Church to draw up its list of active members on the basis of attendance at the Lord's table. But if there is anything more disturbing than the gap between the number of confirmed members and the number of communicants, it is the fact that among the latter are many to whom Communion has meant only an external ecclesiastical rite, not an occasion for genuine self-examination, contrition, and joy in the assurance of forgiveness. Luther himself once expressed the wish that as many as one-tenth of communing Christians would receive the sacrament in living faith as assurance of God's grace instead of degrading it into "sham and mere external show."[3] In a sermon "On the Reception of the Holy Sacrament" in 1523, he even presented the idea that "we are not to cast the sacrament among the people in a crowd, as the pope has done," but "to gather into one place those who truly

---

[3] WA X, III, 48 ff.

believe," and after the believers had strengthened each other by testifying of their faith, they were to receive the sacrament only among themselves without the presence of unbelievers or nominal believers.[4] Recognizing the danger implicit in such exclusiveness, Luther did not attempt to carry out this suggestion, but neither should we lose sight of the still greater danger of lifeless externalism which prompted the suggestion. It is at least an open question: which commits the greater error, the pastor who refuses to admit to Communion anyone except his own people whom he has examined and prepared to receive it worthily, or the pastor who indiscriminately invites everyone, even exhorting his nominal members to come, in order to have a larger communing list, without any attempt through individual soul-care to bring about repentance? The former may be guilty of narrowness, but is not the latter encouraging unbelief and hypocrisy?

What has happened, even in Lutheran churches, to those special practices and precautions by which the character of Holy Communion as the occasion for personal forgiveness of sins has been maintained? The first of these is confession, especially private confession to the pastor. In declaring that abolition of the abuses of the confessional did not mean the abolition of the confessional itself, the Augsburg Confession states: "It is not usual to give the body of the Lord, except to them who have been previously examined and ab-

---

[4] EA XI, 203.

solved" (Art. XXV). Today public confession of a
formal liturgical type has almost entirely supplanted
such soul-care. And often even this liturgical penance
is further toned down by the individual pastor to suit
the convenience of the modern "believer." "Let us
humbly kneel and make confession" reads the Order of
Public Confession in the *Common Service Book,* and
where this form is followed worshipers in many of our
churches have their only opportunity to express contrition by kneeling in the house of God. But where this
rubric is arbitrarily changed to "Let us stand" even this
opportunity is taken away. Since the sacrament is likewise generally received while standing, there are actually many Lutheran churches where one can be a member for decades without once being on his knees before
God. The outward act may appear insignificant, but in
a church which lives by the Gospel of the forgiveness
of sins the attitude it expresses is of first-rate importance. And what about the practice of absolution by the
laying on of hands, of which Luther said: "According
to the ordinance of God, sins are forgiven through the
laying on of hands" and "Thou art, therefore, bound to
believe him (the absolver) as though Christ were standing there himself and would lay his hand upon thee
and pronounce the absolution"?[5] When one has partici-
pated in a confessional service of the Evangelical
Lutheran Church, in which Lutherans of Norwegian
descent have faithfully preserved this sacred heritage,

---
[5] WA XLIX, 148.

he is led to wonder what other Lutherans have gained by allowing so comforting and strengthening an application of the Gospel to fall into disuse. And finally, aside from public confession preparatory to Communion, in how vital a use is "the power of the keys," which, in Luther's words, is "the office, power, or command given by God through Christ to Christendom to forgive men their sins"?[6] It is true that every correct Lutheran service of worship opens with confession and absolution, but to how many worshipers is this a deep spiritual experience in which painful tensions are released as God's healing hand is laid on a bruised soul? Is it not only too often a mere formality void of any personal significance? In how many of our churches is the prevailing atmosphere that of a "fellowship of forgiveness" in which one member unburdens to another the load weighing upon his conscience and receives from him the reassuring word of divine pardon?

It is obvious that if the Gospel is to be taken seriously, it will mean nothing less than a new Reformation within the Church. The Church of the Reformation came into being because the medieval church with all its pomp and ceremony, all its doctrines, rituals, and exercises, could not bring relief to the distressed conscience of a man who asked: How can I take hold of God's grace and obtain personal assurance of His salvation? The answer came not from any formula or performance but from the remarkable discovery that faith can mean, and

---

[6] WA XXX, II, 497.

in its true Christian sense does mean, a direct contact with the redeeming Christ himself. Launched forth with this insight into the Gospel, the evangelical Church has itself in the course of the centuries grown into a powerful and world-wide, if as yet loosely organized, ecclesiastical institution rivaling Rome itself. Even the scandal of disunity is being overcome by an ecumenical movement constantly gaining in strength until an organized and integrated Protestantism is no longer a mere idle dream. While such expansion and organization bring power and prestige to the Church as an institution, it is fraught with grave inner perils. The unity attained may be, as in many a merging of church bodies it has been, not a unity of deepened conviction but one of growing indifference to beliefs which to the fathers were matters of vital importance. Worst of all, attention tends to shift to externals, so that while the form of godliness is maintained and embellished, its soul-changing power is lost. Protestantism is not immune to the tragedy which overtook the Roman church as it exchanged the true treasure of the Church, the Gospel, for outward splendor. We need but recall the story of Pope Urban who prepared for Thomas Aquinas a magnificent display of the wealth and power of the Church. "Thomas," he said, "the Church can no longer say, 'Silver and gold have I none.' " "No," replied Thomas, "but neither can it say, 'Take up thy bed and walk.' " What shall it profit Protestantism if it gain an influence in the affairs of the world surpassing that of Rome, if it lose its own soul, the power to make Christ a living reality in the hearts of individual men?

Since the only source of the saving power of God, the only means by which He gives us Christ, is the Evangel or Gospel, it follows that every phase of the Church's activity must serve the primary purpose of evangelism. In the major Protestant denominations the term has commonly come to signify the attempt to reach the unchurched and to persuade them to become members of the congregations. Since about half the population of this country is still unchurched, it has become clear that the task is too big for the professional clergy alone. Hence the more progressive congregations are seeking to train their laity in the techniques of persuasion to carry on this work on a more extensive scale. When, however, such solicitation is undertaken by the average church member who has no vital personal experience of repentance and faith, it becomes a case of the blind leading the blind. Rehearsed and memorized techniques, although they may be based on the most up-to-date psychology of advertising and selling, will always lack the vital spontaneity of true evangelical soul-winning. And even when the people thus gathered are given formal catechetical instruction, the result is usually the same as in the case of the young confirmands, membership in the organized church, not personal commitment to Christ.

True evangelism means much more than this. It is not only a particular phase or form of the Church's program and it involves not only the canvassing and training of new members. It affords the goal and the motivation for everything the Church does. Bringing people within the sphere of the Church's influence has its place, as does the organizing of adult catechetical classes. So does the rest of the system of religious education, a liturgically correct form of worship, an attractive youth program, and whatever other instrumentality the congregation needs for making and maintaining effective contacts with all classes and ages of people. But the setting up of all this machinery is only preliminary to the real work of the Church. It is at best merely a breaking of the ground, a setting of the stage, a maneuvering for position. The major strategy must always be to confront the men and women and the boys and girls, whose lives the Church touches, with the question of questions phrased thus by Karl Heim: "Is Christ merely a great personality of the past or is He the living Lord of history who can tell me with full authority what I have to do amid all the complicated problems of the present? Jesus the Lord confronts us all with an Either-Or; we must either commit the whole of our life to Him or repudiate Him passionately and completely."[7] Pastors could hardly make a graver mistake or do their congregations a greater injustice than to take for granted that people are Christians because they have been instructed in Christian doctrine and led to participate in the round of congregational activities, without

---

[7] *Jesus der Herr,* Preface.

any such personal confrontation or decision. Vital Christianity does not reside in unawakened consciences and unconverted hearts.

While the larger and more highly institutionalized denominations have tended to settle down to a complacent respectability, the work of evangelizing the masses has been undertaken by the various revivalistic sects and "holiness" groups. Statistics show that it is they which represent the growing edge of Protestantism. In missionary zeal, both at home and abroad, they far outstrip the old churches. It is a striking fact that the "free churches" of Sweden, comprising less than one-tenth of the nation's population, have more foreign missionaries in the field than the established Lutheran church to which more than nine-tenths of the people belong. In spite of its utterly fantastic theology, the fastest growing and most zealous religious group in America today is Jehovah's Witnesses. As in the dying days of the Roman Empire, a wave of emotional religion is sweeping through our crumbling civilization, giving warmth to souls whom the ideologies and the ceremonies of traditional religion have left shivering. It is well to remember that original Christianity, too, like the various mysteries from the East which invaded Rome, made a direct appeal to the feelings and consciences of men. The current sects are a God-sent rebuke to a lifeless church which has lost the power of that appeal. But had not the Gospel of salvation by the blood of the Lamb been shown to possess a sturdier truth-content than the "taurobolium," the exotic blood-bath of the Cybele-Attis cult, it would have had no more permanence than that cult. Emotional frenzy and sanctified ignorance are not enough for lasting results. Using Gibbon's description of the Whirling Dervishes, it is a mistake to confuse "giddiness of the head" with "illumination of the spirit." While large numbers of people are susceptible to such giddiness at certain times, and some people find in it their native atmosphere, an "evangelism" which relies chiefly upon emotional exploitation and brings Christian truth into disrepute among the intelligent is a dangerously superficial version of the Christian Gospel. Sound evangelism requires a sound theology of the Gospel.

Let us observe, then, some of the implications for a true evangelism which are contained in the three foundation-principles of evangelical theology which we have studied. Take first of all the central principle: man is justified before God not by any merits of his own but by the grace of God through faith in Jesus Christ. Here the emphasis is upon Christ, grace, and faith. Above all is the centrality and uniqueness of Christ. To the man who seeks an answer to the pivotal question, "Can I enter into a personal relationship with God in such a way that groping will give way to certainty?" the Gospel presents the incarnate personal Word who says, "I am the way . . . No man cometh to the Father but by me." Religion ceases to be defined in terms of mere generalities, such as values and principles, attitudes and aspirations. It takes on the specific Christian meaning of fellowship with God mediated by Christ. In the center of awareness is not man himself, what he is or hopes to be, but the God who has become real and near in Christ. The second emphasis is grace. It means that the starting-point and constant pivot of the relationship with God is the divine love which forgives sins and makes fellowship possible. The Christ of faith is infinitely more than teacher, lawgiver, and example. He is the Reconciler. He personifies that love which leaves the righteous to their righteousness and prefers to associate with sinners. Here lies the peculiarity of the Gospel, a trait which distinguishes it from all other forms of religion. Common to all forms of human religiosity is the belief that man must make something of himself, develop his latent spiritual potentialities, achieve value of some sort, in order to be acceptable to God. Even in the allegedly "evangelistic" holiness groups the center of gravity unconsciously shifts from God to man and what he has become or may become. It is not uncommon to find among them persons who claim not to have committed any sins for many years and therefore actually to have no further need of a Saviour. An evangelism which is Christ-centered and grace-centered never forgets, "If we say we have no sin, we deceive ourselves" and that the most dangerous form of such self-deception is spiritual pride. Those who live by the Gospel never arrive at the stage where they can afford to skip the petition, "Forgive us our trespasses," for they humbly acknowledge that whatever they do is the work of sinful men and whatever is in them of holiness and righteousness is the gift of grace. And grace is the spontaneous activity of God's own nature, unmotivated and unconditioned by anything in us. As regards the believer's estimate of himself, he is and remains a sinner, but by the grace of God a justified and pardoned sinner. His growth in sanctification consists in a deepening awareness of sin, an increasing appreciation of grace, and hence a growing dependence upon Christ. Thus the third major emphasis is faith, the commitment into the hands of God in the trust that He who has revealed His fatherly heart in Christ "doeth all things well" in life and in death. It is that double movement of eternity, that life of the open palm, of which Kierkegaard speaks, in which a man daily surrenders his life to God, daily to receive it back from Him as a gift, but never encloses possessing fingers around it as though it were his own. Only when a man can thus entrust himself to God does he have unfailing security and strength to serve, for he no longer has to struggle on his own, wavering between pride and despair. He has discovered that life-giving truth which gives evangelical Christianity its mission and its power: "The righteous shall live by faith."

This Gospel is the heart and soul of all true evangelism. It establishes evangelism as the major strategy of the Church both by demonstrating its urgent necessity and by supplying its dynamic. The need of evangelism is directly commensurate with man's need of grace. Until recent years the sense of that need was exceedingly weak, especially among the educated, because sin had been largely explained away. As scientific, evolutionary, and humanistic self-realization supplanted the Christian Gospel of the forgiveness of sins, evangelism gave way to moralistic character-building programs relying upon pragmatic methods. As Dr. Henry Sloane Coffin has expressed it, the question "Wretched man that I am, who will deliver me?" was changed into "Progressive creature that I am, who will help me to evolve myself?" Today the atmosphere is quite different. Thus Fosdick in his famous sermon "Beyond Modernism" was led to exclaim: "My soul, what a world, which the gentle modernism of my younger ministry, with its kindly sentiments and lush optimism, does not fit at all!"[8] What does fit is the Christian truth that man is inextricably involved in sin and that his salvation must come from God. The profounder religious thinkers of the day are indeed beginning to appreciate the depth of Luther's insight that the essential nature of sin is revealed not so much in man's sensuousness or worldliness as in his highest spiritual interests. Even in religion man is "incurvatus in se," huddled up in himself, bent upon realizing his own aims, using God as a means to his ends. Man's natural religiosity thus not only fails to carry him in the direction of God. Being motivated by sinful egocentricity, it carries him all the farther in the

[8] *The Christian Century,* Dec. 4, 1935.

wrong direction. There is no escape from this predicament, except through the grace that comes entirely from the outside, encompasses the sinner in the midst of his sin, and freely gives fellowship with God to the ungodly.

This diagnosis of the human situation has been lacking not only among the churches gently ministering to the educated, but also in the popular evangelism among the masses. While the fire-and-brimstone preaching of the tabernacle "evangelists" has awakened men's fear, it has actually attacked and removed the fear of the consequences of sin rather than penetrated to the roots of sin itself. This type of evangelism is much more proficient in dealing with sins as such than with man as a sinner. It draws up lists of specific sins and attacks them one by one. While it may thus get rid of the outward symptoms, it leaves untouched the underlying inner cause, the wrong orientation which man, even in religion, has toward God. As a consequence the kind of "holiness" it generates is usually characterized less by penitent self-examination and humility than by exaggerated self-importance and pride.

Whether or not evangelism is necessary depends upon the answer to the question: "What can man give as a ransom for his soul?" If man can *give* something, it is unnecessary for God to *forgive*. If man is at any time spiritually solvent, he does not need a Redeemer. But if he has to say, "Nothing in my hand I bring," then he has to say also, "Simply to Thy Cross I cling." The

Gospel of the Cross is an absolute necessity or it is nothing. Only the deep insight into man's sinfulness which marks Paul and Luther and Calvin can give evangelism the note of genuine urgency. A newspaperman, impressed by a Gospel sermon, asked the preacher: "If the churches actually believe what you preach, why aren't they desperate about it?" There is an overtone of that desperateness in Paul's cry, "Woe is me, if I preach not the Gospel!" A dispassionate attitude is utterly incompatible with the nature of the Gospel. A collection of sermons published some years ago bore the title "If I Had Only One Sermon to Preach." Every Gospel sermon has that same earnestness. To use Kierkegaard's phrase, Christianity is the life of the eleventh hour. To be a minister of the Gospel is to be commissioned to deliver divine pardon to doomed men. Our generation, perhaps more than any other, is aware of the inevitability and the imminence of the doom which man's sinful stupidity has occasioned. Men go about their tasks fearful and anxious but "without God and without hope." Churches which in such a day settle down to mere routine are guilty of high treason to the Gospel.

The Gospel of justifying grace not only reveals the urgent necessity of evangelism but it also supplies it with inexhaustible motivating and sustaining power. "Seeing we have this ministry, even as we obtained mercy," says Paul, "we faint not." We "never lose heart in it," as Moffatt translates the "faint not." There is something in the ambassadorship of God's "good news" that impels us forward and keeps us going. The enthusiasms which are drawn from man's emotional resources are soon used up. Weariness and exhaustion set in. The only alternative then left is the legalistic "You must." The obstreperous will is flogged with exhortations: "You must do better," "You must try harder." Sensitive consciences are thus led to despondency, the less sensitive to self-righteousness. With the Gospel of grace the case is entirely different. It is in the indicative, a narrative of what God has done and is doing, not in the imperative, a demand to man to do something.   To admonish people to try harder to be better is no Gospel at all. They do not need a Christian minister simply to tell them that, for they have heard it ever since kindergarten. There is still less Gospel in the admonition to love God, for as Luther discovered, that is Law of the most damning sort. To exhort man who is "by nature sinful and unclean" to love God with his whole heart is truly to try to gather grapes from thorns and figs from thistles. It is as cruel as it is futile. It is like telling a soldier whose legs have been shot off from under him to get up and march. There is a Christian imperative, to be sure, but its "Sin no more" is grounded upon the categorical and unconditioned "Thou art made whole." The gift precedes the task. Good works have vitality, for they are fruits, not tricks. They flow out of a rich fullness and are not eked out of poverty. Grateful love is the secret of doing great things, and forgiveness is the secret of grateful love. As James Denney puts it, "Everyone who knows what it is to be forgiven knows also that forgiveness is the greatest regenerative force in the life of man."[9]

Since the Gospel contains the gift of new life to change the human heart from within, it carries vital power for its own propagation when it is implanted there. This power has certain well-marked traits. The first of these is a joyful spontaneity as contrasted with all legalistic strain and coercion. The more it takes hold of us, the less we have to carry it along, for it carries us along. In Luther's fine phrase, we serve God "hilari et libera voluntate," with a glad and free will. The way of grace is not the way of threats and arguments. It manifests its power by that intrinsic attractiveness and winsomeness which is among the connotations of the rich word "grace" and which is so vividly personified in our Lord himself. Another trait is its outgoing and overflowing quality. Love is not self-contained or close-lipped. It is impelled from within to communicate itself, to share its perfections, to create fellowship. That is why the faith that is born of grace is, as Luther says, "a turbulent thing that cannot but do good." It wins men's hearts by surrounding them with so much sincere and resourceful interest that they must do themselves violence to spurn it. Still another trait is its disregard of barriers. It is no respecter of persons. It draws no distinction even between the worthy and the unworthy,

---

[9] *Christian Doctrine of Reconciliation* (N. Y.: Doran, 1918), p. 6.

the deserving and the undeserving. It does not seek worth but creates worth where it did not exist before. Finally, it does not become discouraged in the face of any apparent failure. It can afford to pour itself out with utter recklessness, seemingly to waste itself upon the undeserving, for it draws upon infinite resources. It may be of the very nature of love, thought Luther, to be rejected and despised and crucified, and yet it manages to carry on, for "love never faileth."

When we turn from the major strategy of evangelism to its specific tactics, and inquire by what means the Gospel of saving grace is to do its work in men's lives, we find the answer in the second basic principle of evangelical theology, the supremacy and normativeness of the Word. The Word in all its forms, written, oral, and visible, is the means of grace. There is no place in the Church, insisted Luther, for a spirituality not mediated by the Word and the Sacraments. The discovery of the Bible meant to him freedom from the conflicting and misleading opinions of men. It meant: God himself speaks. As servants of the Word we are equipped with something more substantial than surmises and theories. We have a definite "kerygma," a proclamation, a commissioned message. Here lies a question of critical importance for all ministers of the Gospel. Is the message we preach and teach and which we ask people to accept truly God's own Word? Can "Thus saith the Lord" honestly be affixed to it, or does it only give voice to men's spiritual needs, desires, and aspirations? According to Canon Theodore Wedel of the Washington Cathedral, "An entire generation or more has grown up, even within the churches, who have never heard the true Christian gospel." If this statement is true, it is the most serious indictment that could be made of the Church. And yet if one listens to some of the popularly acclaimed "great" preachers or reads the volumes of "best sermons," it is difficult to escape this conclusion. The model sermon appears to be a mosaic cleverly fitted together from various sources and apparently meant to be chiefly a performance in good public speaking, having as its primary end the holding of people's interest. Such preaching achieves at best a "prophetic" tone of condemning godlessness and injustice and vindicating the judgments of a righteous God, but rarely leads to the true end of the proclamation of the Word, the faith by which the tendrils of men's hearts cling to Christ. It was said of Sadhu Sundar Singh that having heard him preach men forgot themselves and forgot the preacher and thought only of Christ. It is by that standard that preaching is to be judged.

Sound evangelical preaching is of course scriptural preaching, but in a more significant sense than mere quotation of Scripture or making correct doctrinal statements based on Scripture. I once asked my class in dogmatics to write essays on the theme "What must I do to be saved?" One young man turned in a paper bearing only the appropriate verse of Scripture: "Believe on the Lord Jesus Christ and thou shalt be saved." He was neither lazy nor facetious but an able and conscientious student. After due deliberation he simply decided that there was nothing more to be said on that particular question and hence wasted no words. It was my duty to point out that he had written an admirable first sentence and to encourage him to go on from that point in the same spirit. For while Paul did give this answer to the Philippian jailer, he would hardly have achieved the result which he did, the conversion of the man and of his household, if he had nothing more to say. No passage of Scripture acts as an impersonal magic formula. Scripture becomes the means of grace only when it is accompanied by the same living Spirit who originally inspired its writing, and the Spirit both then and now inspires only persons. Thus even though the student would have learned from his course in Christian doctrine other relevant verses of the Bible and learned also to intersperse them with pure doctrine on the order of salvation, it would not follow that his new and longer essay would achieve the results Paul obtained. To use a rather crude metaphor, the conversion experience resulting from Paul's proclamation of the Word may be represented by the experience of falling in love, in comparison with which the student's essay on the way of salvation might be similar to a treatise on "What a Young Man Ought to Know About Love." Such a treatise has its uses but it is a poor substitute for the reality itself. Religious life will continue to be at a low ebb in our congregations so long as we operate simply on the assumption that vital religion can be taught without stressing that it has to be caught. It is a fallacious idea, drawn from Greek philosophy, not from the Christian Gospel, that correct knowledge will automatically result in right action. He who knew what is in man made His primary appeal not to a man's intellect but to his will: "Wilt thou be made whole?" "What wilt thou that I should do unto thee?" And His greatest apostle was not satisfied with "manifesting the truth." His program was: "By manifesting the truth we commend ourselves to every man's conscience." Teaching men to know the great truths which the Bible teaches about God and man, life and death, sin and salvation, is an indispensable preface to genuine Christianity. But all this remains a dead letter unless the living Word as the sword of the Spirit penetrates men's consciences, "piercing to the division of the soul and the spirit, of joints and marrow, and discerning the thoughts and intentions of the heart" (Heb. 4:12).

How, then, is the Word of God to be applied in order that it may reach men's consciences and bring about repentance and faith? Luther's answer is: rightly "to divide the word of truth" is, first of all, rightly to distinguish between the Law and the Gospel. This, according to the Reformer, is a most difficult art to learn, and one who has learned it is a true Doctor of Theology. The function of the Law, all that content of God's Word which forbids and commands, is to awaken and terrify the sleeping conscience. The preacher of the Word is to present God's righteousness and sovereignty and the seriousness of man's rebellion against God in such an uncompromising way that any who commit sin, after they have heard him, do so with an uneasy conscience. Since every man is by nature a sinner, i.e., there is in him an ineradicable self-centeredness which is opposed to God and His grace, the Law has a permanent function with regard to this "old Adam" or "flesh." The flesh, says Luther, must never be freed from the yoke of the Law. If man's natural self-centered religiosity is allowed free reign, it either perverts the Law into an instrument of salvation, thus leading to self-righteousness, or it uses the Gospel as a cloak of sin. So great was Luther's dread of an antinomian abuse of the Gospel that he was led to insist: even Roman Catholic penance, with all its errors, is better than no penance at all. Judged by God's Law, we realize that sin is something more than a failure to live up to our ideals. The ideals themselves are corrupt. Before the bar of divine judgment our virtues as well as our vices stand in need of forgiveness.

But the constructive aspect of salvation, saving faith and the power of a new life, is entirely a matter of the Gospel, the proclamation of free unmerited grace in Christ, from which every element of legalistic coercion must be removed. There is not a single problem of our relation to God which does not have its ultimate positive solution in Christ. Thus even the contrition which the Law works in us leads to true repentance only in the presence of Him who in this respect also fulfills the Law. Following Luther's advice, "It is the preaching of God's judgment and wrath that works repentance," we may have attempted in vain to awaken in the self-satisfied people we have to work with a sense of spiritual need. We may have concluded that this generation, which is said to be familiar at sixteen with more deviltry than their grandparents ever knew, evidently cannot be frightened with the pronouncements of judgment and wrath which struck terror into the hearts of people in Luther's day. Is there, then, any way in which we can produce in the people of our day that consciousness of sin which will lead them to accept and appreciate the Gospel of forgiveness? The final answer must be in the Christ in whom are hid *all* the treasures of wisdom and knowledge. When He tells men the truth about themselves it is all the more effective because it is truth spoken in love. Like the poor paralytic of the gospel story, men and women of today can do nothing, not even repent, until loving hands have carried them to Christ and they have heard His voice. In spite of his skirmishes with the Law, Paul was still a proud Pharisee who confessed to no wrongdoing and acknowledged no spiritual need until he found himself face to face with the pardoning Saviour. He never recovered from his amazement at the mysterious love that sought him out while he was still indifferent, and even worse than that, an enemy. He had no defense against the Christ who

loved him and died for him while he was still hostile.
It was against the background of that kind of love that
his unbelief became manifest in all its sinfulness. The
Cross is the strongest word of judgment as it is of redemption. It both convicts and pardons. This result will
not, of course, be achieved in every case. Man's sinful
self-will may frustrate God's redeeming will, so that
grace, as far as he is concerned, is in vain. But until a
man has "passionately and completely" spurned Christ,
we dare not give him up as lost. Our ministry of reconciliation has its limits to be sure. Nygrén is right in saying, "That which cannot be won by the reckless self-
giving of love cannot be won at all; there remains only
judgment."[10] We may well ask, however, whether we
are ever in position to apply that word to any given
individual. Our proper question is: How fully have we
explored and how resourcefully have we applied the
soul-winning power of Christ?

Uniquely important in the application of the Gospel
is individual soul-care. The gospels make it plain that
it was by the use of this method that our Lord himself
was most successful in winning men's hearts. The
crowds who heard Him were often fickle and forgetful,
misunderstanding His teachings and even turning
against Him in anger. But His interviews with individuals such as Zacchaeus, Nicodemus, the woman of
Samaria, and many others, those perfect masterpieces

---

[10] *Agape and Eros*, tr. A. G. Hebert (London: S.P.C.K., 1932),
I, 75.

of personal counseling, constitute a remarkable series of object-lessons in soul-winning. Souls are not saved in bundles, and while people may have deserted Christ en masse, they must be led back to Him one by one. Since the minister of the Gospel aims at nothing less than a spontaneous whole-hearted commitment ensuing in a devoted life-partnership with God, his methods cannot be those of a journeyman revivalist who must show concrete results from a week or two of emotional "blitzkrieg" or lose face. We cannot try to sweep people off their feet through persuasive eloquence and the power of suggestion. Cunning artifice and concentrated assault may be effective methods for overriding opposition; they are not the way to make or keep friends. The get-rich-quick attitude is not the soil, nor high-pressure coercion the method of cultivation, for growing Christian personality. Nor are mass methods of the indoctrinating type an adequate alternative. As we have already noted, while they may succeed in increasing external church membership, they tend to by-pass vital personal Christianity. We can most effectively lead men to Christ when we have personal knowledge of their individual needs, their unique backgrounds and behavior-patterns, and their concrete life-problems. Such knowledge of men enables us not only to preach "to their condition" but also to make a direct person-to-person application of the Word through private conversation.

The best modern psychotherapy has served to cor-

roborate both the essential content of the Gospel and
the effectiveness of individual soul-care as the instrument for its application. The deep-seated and destructive force of sin and the constructive power of forgiveness, the futility of man's own effort and the need of
tapping sources of strength outside himself, these basic
doctrines now appear more vital than ever. Particular
importance as a therapeutic agency attaches to that
Christian variety of the psychoanalytic method known
as the confessional. Confession means, as William
James pointed out, a general purgation of the inner
life, an opportunity "to exteriorize our rottenness." Hidden conflicts are brought to light, and the sinner is
enabled to face his wrong without camouflage. Luther
with his keen sense for what is vital in religion placed
tremendous emphasis upon private confession. "The
devil would have slain me long ago," he says, "had not
confession sustained me."[11] His advice to others is
therefore: "Let every Christian when the devil attacks
him and suggests that he is a great sinner and he must
be lost and condemned . . . not long contend with him
or remain alone, but go or call his pastor, or any other
good friend, lay his trouble before him, and seek coun-
sel and comfort from him, and remain firm in what
Christ declares: 'Whose soever sins ye remit, they are
remitted unto them' . . . and whatever this person says
to him in the name of Christ from the Scriptures, let
him believe it, and according to his faith it shall be

[11.] WA X, III, 61.

done unto him."[12] Protestantism has had to pay a heavy price for its apostasy from the spiritual values contained in the confessional. The psychiatrist and the Christian Science practitioner, besides quacks of all kinds, have taken over the functions neglected by the pastor. "Confess your sins to one another," says the Word (James 5:16). There is no substitute for the methods which the Word itself offers for the application of the Gospel to the hearts of men.

It remains for us to bring to mind the significance of the third of the basic principles of evangelical theology, the spiritual priesthood of all believers, for the Church's task of evangelization. Here we can afford to be quite brief, for, as we have observed in the preceding chapter, the principle itself represents the evangelical faith at work. Its implications as a broad program of action have therefore already been noted. What a revolution it would mean in our churches if the dynamic conception of church membership contained in this principle were once more to prevail in its original power! No more would people hold the utterly unevangelical idea that once they have united with the congregation they have done their duty when they attend the services and carry their share of the budget with which a man is hired to keep the organization running. And in asking men and women to work for God's Kingdom we would give them nobler tasks to perform than merely ushering people to the pews, taking up the offering, or enter-

---

[12] WA XLIX, 147.

taining the Ladies' Aid. What if every member recognized his status as a member of a messianic royal priesthood and accepted as a sacred privilege his responsibility to be a missionary and an evangelist? And what if the "service" performed within the fellowship were to consist primarily in what Luther terms "the greatest service I can render my neighbor," namely, by using the power of the keys which Christ has given to every Christian "to release from sin, to deliver from the devil and hell" the conscience of a fellow-Christian?[13] What if "preaching" were to be something more than a set twenty-minute public performance by one member of the fellowship and were to take on the added connotation which Luther gives it when he speaks of a private conversation between two church members in these terms: "I preach the Gospel to a person and tell him to appropriate the words of Christ and to believe firmly that Christ's righteousness is his own, and his sins are Christ's."[14] In a word, what if the essential purpose of church membership meant to us what it meant to Luther: "Christ has ordained us all to be priests, in order that one may proclaim to the other the forgiveness of sins"?[15]

Such a view of the Church as a fellowship of forgiveness in which each member is consecrated to lift the burden of sins from the conscience of another and to

---

[13] EA XI, 346.

[14] *Ibid.*

[15] WA XLIX, 150.

strengthen him in grace provides also new depth and power to the concept of Christian service to the community and the world at large. It broadens the range and vitalizes the content of Christian witness-bearing by consecrating every Christian to this task and giving him a message drawn from living experience. And since this witness-bearing takes place, as we observed in Chapter IV, within the divinely appointed frameworks of life and in the setting of one's daily calling, universal spiritual priesthood enables the Church to exert its influence in all human contacts and to reach men not by mere institutionalized canvasses from time to time but by the continuous and matchlessly effective medium of person-to-person communication wherever "cross the crowded ways of life." People become the objects not of an impersonal ecclesiastical program but of sincere personal interest on the part of men with whom they associate. The deepest personal needs of a man are best met not by a technique but by a friend. Dr. Coffin's definition of a pastor, "a friend at large," should apply to every Christian. And the Gospel of divine friendship by which a Christian lives and to which he bears witness does minister to a man's deepest needs. Others may help him to improve the external conditions of life, but Christ alone can forgive his sins and give him new life in fellowship with God.

Such, then, is the heart of the evangelical faith in the contemporary scene and in every scene: the grace of God in Jesus Christ, an immeasurable depth of redemptive love which alone is more than a match for the depth of human tragedy and provides saving resources from a realm beyond all human achievement; the eternal Word through which men personally confront God's judgment and mercy; and the fellowship of believers, created and sustained by the Word to serve as the instrument of the divine redeeming purpose. God's victory over sin will become manifest, in increasing measure, in the lives of individual men and women and in the life of humanity as a whole, as the Church becomes rededicated to that purpose through the resurgence of the living Gospel. And this Gospel will exert its transforming power in every human situation as every Christian becomes a fisher of men who learns to say in faith, even when earthly signs point only to despair: "Nevertheless at thy word I will."

Type used in this book
Body, 11 on 14 and 10 on 12 Caledonia
Display, Bodoni bold

INDEX